MW00464574

FAIRYTALE BAKING

Christin Geweke

Fairytale Baking

Delicious Treats Inspired by Snow White, Hansel & Gretel, and Other Classic Stories

Photography by Yelda Yilmaz

Skyhorse Publishing

CONTENTS

PREFACE

ONCE UPON A TIME, MANY MOONS AGO, there was a little girl who discovered her love for baking. I was not even four years old and absolutely entranced by my mother mixing and kneading all sorts of different doughs and batters. I loved to help her cut cookies and – oh, the sheer delight of it! – to wipe the various bowls clean with my fingers afterwards, licking streaks of melted chocolate, little mounds of whipped vanilla cream and sticky batters off them. My cheeks still dusty with flour, I would then sit cross-legged in front of the oven, entirely transfixed. I would watch batters and doughs fluff up and rise and change color like magic, slowly baking to perfection and filling our entire home with an irresistible aroma. And then, as soon as our little silver kitchen timer beeped, my eager anticipation would reach its climax, as I knew I would be allowed to try the finished, still hot cake. Just a tiny piece. And maybe another one. Full of pride. These moments were imbued with a magic that delighted all of my senses and are among my fondest memories. They bring up memories of warmth and belonging – like snuggling up to hear a fairytale.

My mother inherited her passion for baking from her own mother, my grandmother Frida, who kept her hand-written recipes in an old leather box: recipes for pumpkin bread, red wine cake and so much more. Recipes from a different time. They may no longer be fashionable but they still work as they have always done. Every time. And what's most important is that they taste reassuringly the same – every time. They transport young and old to a different world, a world beyond the stresses of everyday life.

Like old family recipes, fairytales are also handed down from one generation to the next. For centuries, wide-eyed children have been sitting on their mothers' and fathers' laps and holding hands with their siblings or grandparents, being entranced by fantastic, exciting stories about poor stepdaughters, courageous orphans, despotic kings and rebellious princes. What makes these ancient tales so beautiful is not just that they invariably have a happy ending, but that they keep being told and read from one generation to the next, creating closeness and warmth through shared excitement.

And delicious baking can delight the senses just like a good story, regardless of people's age. Baking together can be a beautiful, harmonious experience, but the best is, of course, the shared feast that comes afterwards in a different sort of happy ending. What could be better than to sit around a richly set coffee table with loved ones and indulge in moist pies, sumptuous cakes and other delicacies? These are the kinds of recipes gathered in this book, which marries exquisite classics with contemporary ingredients. These recipes not only look amazing, but are utterly delicious.

My aim was to write recipes that bring up childhood memories, just like the fairytales in this book. But what would delight me most would be if these recipes led to new memories being created. This is what I hope for all readers, most of all for my own children, who have been following the goings-on in our kitchen over the past weeks and months very closely, with wide eyes and very sticky fingers.

I hope this book will bring you plenty of enjoyment through reading, baking, feasting and indulging!

TIPS AND TRICKS

The recipes in this book are aimed at beginners just as much as at experienced bakers. They vary not only in their flavors, but also in their levels of difficulty. Usually, the length of the recipe is a good guideline for its complexity. Read on for some helpful hints to make sure that nothing will stand between you and your personal baking bliss.

Basic ingredients and how to substitute them

Many pies and cakes are easily prepared with just a few staple ingredients you will most likely have in your pantry. But even if you have run out of something or other, there is no need to drop everything to go to the supermarket. Most of the recipes in this book can be happily modified to your taste (or pantry situation) – feel free to experiment.

FLOUR:
While flour is an essential ingredients in many recipes, a substantial amount can usually be substituted for ground nuts (up to 25% of the total quantity). Either use ground nuts from the supermarket such as ground hazelnuts or almonds, or grind them yourself if you have a powerful food processor or blender. Do try out different blends of cashews, macadamias, pecans or other nuts to find your personal favorite. Ground nuts give doughs and batters a particularly rich aroma, but note that they absorb quite a bit of liquid, so increase the liquid ingredients somewhat if you substitute nuts for flour. For an enticingly different flavor, try using roasted, salted nuts, which go surprisingly well with sweet doughs and batters (for example Salted Peanut Cupcakes, see page 100, or White Chocolate Caramel Cake, see page 103). Most of the recipes in this book use plain white flour, which can be replaced with spelt or wholemeal flour if you have run out. Again, you may need to adjust the quantity of the liquid ingredients, since wholemeal flour absorbs more liquid.

SUGAR:
Personally, I love using unrefined raw cane sugar, but I decided against specifying any particular type of sugar in the recipes, as different sugars do not have a major impact on whether a recipe works or not – as long as you do not try to substitute sugar using the same quantity of alternative liquid sweeteners such as honey, agave syrup, rice malt syrup or maple

syrup. Of course, using different types of sugar will have an effect on the taste and sweetness of your baking. I invite you to experiment, but make sure that the proportion of dry and liquid ingredients remains the same. Why not try muscovado or coconut sugar for a different, more aromatic flavor? Dried fruit such as dates makes another lovely and, above all, natural sweetener that creates its own unique taste sensation.

DAIRY PRODUCTS:
I love using any type of dairy products, because they make beautifully creamy pies and cakes. Again, products can be substituted depending on the consistency required: vary between crème fraîche and heavy sour cream, for example, or between mascarpone and heavy cream, or buttermilk and a mixture of full-fat milk and a little plain yogurt. If you are allergic to dairy, feel free to substitute lactose-free products. Many of the recipes can be made suitable for vegans by using soy, rice, coconut or nut milks. Enjoy experimenting with different alternatives!

FATS:
Butter can be substituted with margarine in most recipes, even though the flavor will be different, but I do recommend making shortbread and puff pastries with butter only. Some recipes additionally require a neutral vegetable oil, for example for deep-frying (see page 10). Good choices include sunflower or canola oil, which have a high smoke point. Coconut oil is another oil that can be heated to high temperatures. I also like to add small amounts of coconut oil to melted chocolate or cooking chocolate for icings and glazes, because it gives a beautiful gloss.

Equipment

Professional food processors and kitchen mixers obviously make kitchen work easier. But if you don't bake bread every other day, have a strong passion for meringue or frequently grind nuts, your everyday baking needs will be perfectly covered by just a few basic kitchen aids such as a good old hand mixer. The following are essentials, though:

- various mixing bowls
- precision kitchen scales, ideally digital scales
- a dough scraper, whisk, wooden spoon, slotted spoon and vegetable peeler
- a rolling pin
- cookie cutters of various sizes
- a piping bag with various nozzles (alternatively, use a freezer bag with a corner cut off)
- a kitchen grater
- measuring cups and jugs

The recipes in this book use the following baking tins and trays:

- various springform tins: 18 cm (7 inch), 20 cm (8 inch), 24 cm (9½ inch), 26 cm (10½ inch)
- various pie dishes, ideally with a removable base: 20 cm (8 inch), 24 cm (9½ inch)
- tartlet tins: 10 cm (4 inch)
- loaf tins: 24 cm (9½ inch), 25 cm (10 inch)
- a 12-hole muffin tin
- a 12-hole mini kugelhopf tin
- a kugelhopf tin
- an ovenproof frying pan

Naturally, there is no need to buy every tin and tray in every size, as baking recipes are easily converted. Use the table below as a guide. The left column shows the tin or tray size given in the recipe, while the top row shows the tin or tray size you wish to prepare. Simply multiply or divide the ingredients given in the recipe by the factor shown to keep the ratio between ingredients consistent. Remember to increase or shorten baking times accordingly!

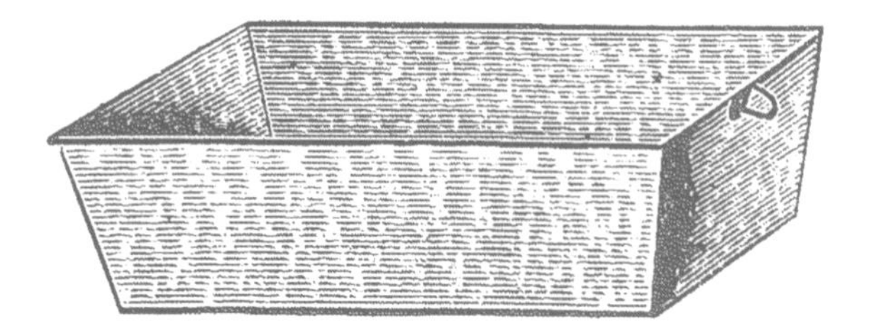

Recipe tin size	Target size			
	18 cm	**20 cm**	**24 cm**	**26 cm**
18 cm		x 1.23	x 1.78	x 2.09
20 cm	x 0.81		x 1.44	x 1.69
24 cm	x 0.56	x 0.69		x 1.17
26 cm	x 0.48	x 0.59	x 0.85	

Oven

Because each oven is different, the temperatures and baking times stated in the recipes can only ever serve as a guide. The information given refers to conventional ovens (not fan-forced), unless stated otherwise. If you are in doubt as to whether your masterpiece has finished baking, use a toothpick to test for doneness: insert a wooden toothpick or thin wooden skewer into the thickest part of the cake and remove again. If it comes out clean, the cake is done. If not, return the cake to the oven and test again after a few more minutes.

Deep-frying

Not all recipes in this book are baked in the oven. Some are deep-fried for a particularly flavorful result (for example the Chocolate Rolls with Apricot Sauce, see page 107, or the Plum Jam Doughnuts, see page 36). There is no need to buy a special deep-fryer for this. Simply use an ordinary saucepan and add enough oil (see also 'Fats' on page 9) to make sure the batter will not touch the base. An oil thermometer may be a useful purchase if you deep-fry regularly. If the oil is not hot enough, the batter does not turn delightfully crispy, but turns soggy and heavy instead. Conversely, if the oil is too hot, your food will brown too quickly on the outside before it is cooked all the way through. The required temperature differs between recipes, but is generally around 170°C (338°F). If you do not have a cooking thermometer, dip a long wooden skewer into the hot oil. The oil is hot enough if small bubbles start to rise quickly. Also, be careful not to deep-fry too many pieces at once, as this will cause the oil temperature to drop excessively. Finally, make sure you leave enough room for turning the pieces with a slotted spoon so that both sides are cooked evenly. Carefully remove the pieces with a slotted spoon when they are done and transfer them to a plate lined with paper towel for draining off excess oil.

Two more important final notes on deep-frying: never allow hot oil to come into contact with water. For example, avoid rinsing your slotted spoon under water and immersing it again into the hot oil without drying it first – this will cause the oil to splatter dangerously. And never pour deep-frying oil down the sink, as this can cause blockages.

Melting chocolate

Chocolate plays the lead role in many recipes, either in the form of cocoa, which gives doughs and batters a rich, dark color, or in the form of melted chocolate for fillings or glazes. Getting the temperature right is essential when melting chocolate, as this determines its gloss and texture. To melt, coarsely chop the chocolate and transfer it to a metal bowl, setting aside a third. Place the bowl over a saucepan of simmering water and gently heat, stirring continuously. Be careful not to allow any water to come into contact with the chocolate or to let the water get too hot, which makes chocolate bitter. The optimal temperature for melting chocolate is about 45°C (113°F). Once the chocolate in the bowl has melted, stir in the remaining third. This reduces the temperature of the melted chocolate to about 28°C (82°F). Gently reheat the mixture to about 32°C (90°F), until all of the chocolate has melted to produce a glossy sheen. This is also the perfect temperature for processing the melted chocolate as required in your chosen recipe.

Fruit – fresh or frozen?

Baking with fruit has many benefits: not only do results look beautifully colorful on serving platters, they also taste amazing and help keep a guilty conscience at bay. After all, you are not simply indulging in a sweet, you are also having a lot of vitamins. However, most fruit is very seasonal, unless you want to buy imported alternatives. Yet, many fruit varieties can be easily substituted by whatever is currently available from your local farmers' market. With berries in particular, it hardly matters which of these tasty little morsels you use in your recipe. Of course it will change the taste, but you may actually discover your favorite berry through seasonal experiments. Frozen products are always a good alternative to fresh fruit, especially in fruit coulis or recipes where the fruit is baked in the oven and therefore loses its shape anyway. If you are using frozen fruit, defrost and drain it thoroughly, or add it frozen to the dough or batter.

Yeast

I use only fresh yeast in the recipes in this book, for example the Chocolate Ring (page 121). I prefer fresh yeast to dried because it tastes better, but dried yeast works just as well and has a long shelf life of several months. Chances are, therefore, that you will have it in your pantry if you spontaneously decide to bake fresh rolls on a Sunday morning. As a rule of thumb, 1 packet dried yeast is equivalent to half a cube of fresh yeast, i.e. 21 g (¾ oz) fresh yeast can be replaced by 7 g (¼ oz) dried yeast. The required quantity for 500 g (1 lb 2 oz) flour is usually half a cube of fresh yeast. If you prefer a less yeasty taste, use somewhat less and leave the dough to rise longer. The more experience you gain with preparing yeast doughs, the more confident you will become in your experiments.

Gelatine

Some recipes in this book use gelatine for setting pie fillings and cream mixtures. Gelatine is a natural gelling agent and thickener that can be a little tricky to process. I suggest you closely follow the instructions below. Gelatine is available in powdered and leaf form. I tend to use only white leaf gelatine. The amount you need will depend on the amount of liquid that you need to set. You will need about 6 leaves of gelatine to set 2 cups (500 ml) liquid, depending on how firm you would like the mixture to be.

First, place the leaves in cold water to soak. It is best to place them into the soaking bowl separately, one after the other, to prevent them from sticking together. Make sure that all leaves are covered with water. After about 5 minutes they should be soft enough. Use your hands to squeeze out the excess water. If you are planning to set a cold mixture, heat a small saucepan over low heat, adding a little liquid, depending on the recipe. Add the squeezed gelatine and melt, stirring continuously. Be careful not to heat the gelatine too much, as this will mean that it will not set. Next, stir in 2–3 tablespoons of the cold mixture you wish to set to even out the temperature between the hot, liquid gelatine and the cold mixture. Stirring hot gelatine straight into a large amount of cold mixture causes clumps. Quickly whisk the warm gelatine mixture from the saucepan into the remaining mixture in your bowl until well combined. Refrigerate the mixture until set – this may take several hours, depending on its volume.

If you wish to set a hot mixture, whisk the soaked, squeezed gelatine leaves straight into the mixture to dissolve, again being careful not to heat the mixture excessively. Never allow gelatine mixtures to simmer! Remove from the heat as soon as the gelatine has dissolved. Leave to cool and then refrigerate until fully set.

A vegetarian and vegan alternative to gelatine is agar flakes, a seaweed product that is also entirely neutral in taste and can be used in a way similar to gelatine to set creams and fillings. However, the various products on the market need to be prepared differently, require different ratios and have different gelling properties. As a result, the outcome may be variable. Always prepare agar flakes according to the instructions on the packet.

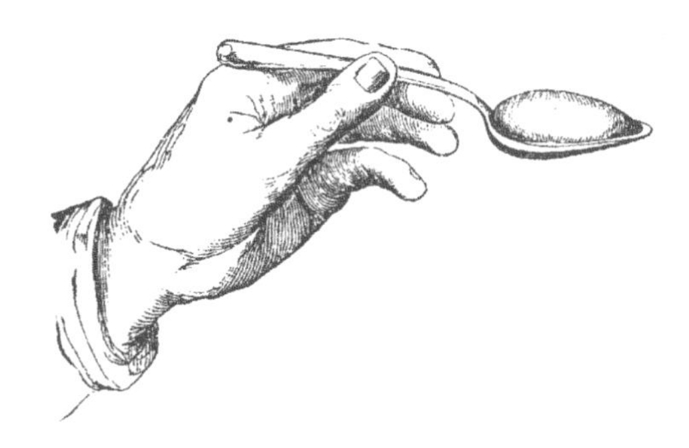

OVEN GUIDE: You may find cooking times vary depending on the oven you are using. For fan-forced ovens, as a general rule, set the oven temperature to 20°C (70°F) lower than indicated in the recipe.

MEASURES GUIDE: We have used 20 ml (4 teaspoon) tablespoon measures. If you are using a 15 ml (3 teaspoon) tablespoon add an extra teaspoon of the ingredient for each tablespoon specified.

Snow-white and Rose-red

CLASSIC BEAUTIES

SNOW-WHITE AND ROSE-RED

There was once a poor widow who lived in a lonely cottage.

In front of the cottage was a garden wherein stood two rose-trees, one of which bore white roses and the other bore red roses. She had two children who were like the two rose-trees; one was called Snow-white, and the other Rose-red. They were as good and happy, as busy and cheerful as ever two children in the world were, only Snow-white was more quiet and gentle than Rose-red. Rose-red liked better to run about in the meadows and fields seeking flowers and catching butterflies; but Snow-white sat at home with her mother and helped her with her housework, or read to her when there was nothing to do.

The two children were so fond of one another that they always held each other by the hand when they went out together, and when Snow-white said: 'We will not leave each other,' Rose-red answered: 'Never so long as we live,' and their mother would add: 'What one has she must share with the other.'

They often ran about the forest alone and gathered red berries, and no beasts did them any harm, but came close to them trustfully. The little hare would eat a cabbage-leaf out of their hands, the doe grazed by their side, the stag leapt merrily by them, and the birds sat still upon the boughs and sang whatever they knew.

No mishap overtook the children; if they had stayed too late in the forest and night came on, they laid themselves down near one another upon the moss and slept until morning came. Their mother knew this and did not worry on their account.

Once when they had spent the night in the wood and the dawn had roused them, they saw a beautiful child in a shining white dress sitting nearby. He got up and looked quite kindly at them, but said nothing and went into the forest. And when they looked around they found that they had been sleeping quite close to a precipice, and would certainly have fallen into it in the darkness if they had gone only a few paces further. Their mother told them that the child they had seen must have been the angel who watches over good children.

Snow-white and Rose-red kept their mother's little cottage so neat that it was a pleasure to look inside it. In the summer Rose-red took care of the house, and every morning laid a wreath of flowers by her mother's bed before she awoke, in which was a rose from each tree. In the winter Snow-white lit the fire and hung the kettle on the hob. The kettle was of brass and shone like gold, so brightly was it polished. In the evening, when the snowflakes fell, the mother said: 'Go, Snow-white, and bolt the door,' and then they sat around the hearth while the mother took her spectacles and read aloud from a large book. The two girls listened as they sat and spun. Close by them lay a lamb upon the floor, and behind them upon a perch sat a white dove with its head hidden beneath its wings.

One evening, as they were thus sitting comfortably together, someone knocked at the door as if he wished to be let in. The mother said: 'Quick, Rose-red, open the door. It must be a traveller who is seeking shelter.' Rose-red went and pushed back the bolt, thinking that it was a poor man, but it was not; it was a bear that stretched his broad, black head within the door.

'QUICK, ROSE-RED, OPEN THE DOOR. IT MUST BE A TRAVELLER SEEKING SHELTER.'

Rose-red screamed and sprang back, the lamb bleated, the dove fluttered, and Snow-white hid herself behind her mother's bed. But the bear began to speak and said: 'Do not be afraid, I will do you no harm! I am half-frozen, and only want to warm myself a little beside you.'

'Poor bear,' said the mother, 'lie down by the fire, only take care that you do not burn your coat.' Then she cried: 'Snow-white, Rose-red, come out. The bear will do you no harm; he means well.' So they both came out, and by-and-by the lamb and dove came nearer, and were not afraid of him. The bear said: 'Here, children, knock the snow out of my coat a little'; so they brought the broom and swept the bear's hide clean; and he stretched himself by the fire and growled contentedly and comfortably. It was not long before they grew quite comfortable, and played tricks with their clumsy guest. They tugged his hair with their hands, put their feet upon his back and rolled him about, or they took a hazel-switch and beat him, and when he growled they laughed. But the bear took it all in good humour, only when they were too rough he called out:

'Leave me alive, children.
Snow-white, Rose-red,
Will you beat your wooer dead?'

When it was bed-time, and the others went to bed, the mother said to the bear: 'You can lie there by the hearth, and then you will be safe from the cold and the bad weather.' As soon as day dawned the two children let him out, and he trotted across the snow into the forest.

Henceforth the bear came every evening at the same time, laid himself down by the hearth, and let the children amuse themselves with him as much as they liked; and they got so used to him that the doors were never fastened until their black friend had arrived.

When spring had come and all outside was green, the bear said one morning to Snow-white: 'Now I must go away, and cannot come back for the whole summer.' 'Where are you going, then, dear bear?' asked Snow-white. 'I must go into the forest and guard my treasures from the wicked dwarfs. In the winter, when the earth is frozen hard, they are obliged to stay below and cannot work their way through; but now, when the sun has thawed and warmed the earth, they break through it, and come out to pry and steal. What once gets into their hands, and into their caves, does not easily see daylight again.'

Snow-white was quite sorry at his departure. As she unbolted the door for him and the bear was hurrying out, he caught against the bolt and a piece of his hairy coat was torn off. It seemed to Snow-white as if she had seen gold shining through it, but she was not sure about it. The bear ran away quickly, and was soon out of sight behind the trees.

A short time afterwards the mother sent her children into the forest to get firewood. There they found a big tree that lay felled on the ground, and close by the trunk something was jumping backwards and forwards in the grass, but they could not make out what it was. When they came nearer they saw a dwarf with an old withered face and a snow-white beard a yard long. The end of the beard was caught in a crevice of the tree, and the little fellow was jumping about like a dog tied to a rope, and did not know what to do.

He glared at the girls with his fiery red eyes and cried: 'Why do you stand there? Can you not come here and help me?' 'What are you up to, little man?' asked Rose-red. 'You stupid, prying goose!' answered the dwarf: 'I was going to split the tree to get a little wood for cooking. The little bit of food that we people get is immediately burnt up with heavy logs; we do not swallow so much as you coarse, greedy folk. I had just driven the wedge in, and everything was going as I wished; but the cursed wedge was too smooth and suddenly sprang out, and the tree closed so quickly that I could not pull out my beautiful white beard. Now it is tight and I cannot get away, and the silly, sleek, milk-faced things laugh! Ugh! How odious you are!'

The children tried very hard, but they could not pull the beard out; it was caught too fast. 'I will run and fetch someone,' said Rose-red. 'You senseless goose!' snarled the dwarf. 'Why should you fetch someone? You are already two too many for me; can you not think of something better?' 'Don't be impatient,' said Snow-white, 'I will help you.' And she pulled her scissors out of her pocket, and cut off the end of the beard.

As soon as the dwarf felt himself free he laid hold of a bag that lay amongst the roots of the tree, and which was full of gold, and lifted it up, grumbling to himself: 'Uncouth people, to cut off a piece of my fine beard. Bad luck to you!' And he swung the bag upon his back, and went off without even once looking at the children.

Some time afterwards, Snow-white and Rose-red went to catch a dish of fish. As they came near the brook they saw something like a large grasshopper jumping towards the water, as if it were going to leap in. They ran to it and found it was the dwarf. 'Where are you going?' asked Rose-red. 'You surely don't want to go into the water?' 'I am not such a fool!' cried the dwarf. 'Don't you see that the accursed fish wants to pull me in?' The little man had been sitting there fishing, and unluckily the wind had tangled up his beard with the fishing-line; a moment later a big fish made a bite and the feeble creature had not strength to pull it out. The fish kept the upper hand and pulled the dwarf towards him. He held on to all the reeds and rushes, but it was of little good, for he was forced to follow the movements of the fish, and was in urgent danger of being dragged into the water.

The girls came just in time. They held him and tried to free his beard from the line, but all in vain; beard and line were entangled fast together. There was nothing to do but to bring out the scissors and cut the beard, whereby a small part of it was lost. When the dwarf saw, he screamed out: 'Is that civil, you toadstool, to disfigure a man's face? Was it not enough to clip off the end of my beard? Now you have cut off the best part of it. I cannot let myself be seen by my people. I wish you had been made to run the soles off your shoes!' Then he took out a sack of pearls that lay in the rushes, and without another word he dragged it away and disappeared behind a stone.

It happened that soon afterwards the mother sent the two children to the town to buy needles and thread, and laces and ribbons. The road led them across a heath upon which huge pieces of rock lay strewn about. There they noticed a large bird hovering in the air, flying slowly round and round above them; it sank lower and lower, and at last settled near a rock not far away. Immediately they heard a loud, piteous cry.

'UNCOUTH PEOPLE, TO CUT OFF A PIECE OF MY FINE BEARD.'

They ran up and saw with horror that the eagle had seized their old acquaintance the dwarf, and was going to carry him off.

The children, full of pity, at once took tight hold of the little man, and pulled against the eagle so long that at last he let his booty go. As soon as the dwarf had recovered from his fright he cried with his shrill voice: 'Could you not have done it more carefully? You dragged at my brown coat so that it is all torn and full of holes, you clumsy creatures!' Then he took up a sack full of precious stones, and slipped away again under the rock into his hole. The girls, who by this time were used to his ingratitude, went on their way and did their business in town.

As they crossed the heath again on their way home they surprised the dwarf, who had emptied out his bag of precious stones in a clearing, and had not thought that anyone would come there so late. The evening sun shone upon the brilliant stones; they glittered and sparkled with all colors so beautifully that the children stood still and stared at them. 'Why do you stand gaping there?' cried the dwarf, and his ashen-grey face became copper-red with rage. He was still cursing when a loud growling was heard, and a black bear came trotting towards them out of the forest. The dwarf sprang up in a fright, but he could not reach his cave, for the bear was already close. With his heart full of dread, he cried: 'Dear Mr Bear, spare me. I will give you all my treasures; look, the beautiful jewels lying there! Grant me my life; what do you want with such a slender little fellow as I? You would not feel me between your teeth. Come, take these two wicked girls. They are tender morsels for you, fat as young quails; for mercy's sake, eat them!' The bear took no heed of his words, but gave the wicked creature a single blow with his paw, and he did not move again.

The girls had run away, but the bear called to them: 'Snow-white and Rose-red, do not be afraid; wait, I will come with you.' Then they recognised his voice and waited, and when he came up to them his bearskin suddenly fell off, and he stood there a handsome man, clothed all in gold. 'I am a king's son,' he said, 'and I was bewitched by that wicked dwarf, who had stolen my treasures; I have had to run about the forest as a savage bear until I was freed by his death. Now he has got his well-deserved punishment.'

Snow-white was married to the prince, and Rose-red to his brother, and they divided between them the great treasure that the dwarf had gathered together in his cave. The old mother lived peacefully and happily with her children for many years. She took the two rose-trees with her, and they stood before her window, and every year bore the most beautiful roses, white and red.

LIGHT SACHERTORTE

MAKES ONE 20 CM (8 INCH) CAKE

175 g (6 oz) white cooking chocolate
6 large eggs, separated
⅔ cup (140 g) sugar
1½ tbsp vanilla sugar
⅔ cup (155 g) butter, softened
¼ cup (35 g) icing (confectioners') sugar
140 g (5 oz) plain flour

For the icing:
1 gelatine sheet
175 g (6 oz) milk cooking chocolate
140 ml (4½ fl oz) single (pure) cream

Also:
Butter, for greasing
About ⅔ cup (225 g) apricot jam (or sieved raspberry or strawberry jam)

1 Preheat the oven to 190°C (375°F). Line the base of a 20 cm (8 inch) springform tin with baking paper. Butter the side of the tin.

2 Coarsely chop the white cooking chocolate. Melt in a heatproof bowl over a saucepan of simmering water, then set aside to cool a little. Whisk the egg whites until semi-stiff. Gradually whisk in the sugar and vanilla sugar. Continue whisking until firm, glossy peaks form. In a separate bowl, whisk the butter and icing sugar until light and creamy, then gradually add the egg yolks. Whisk in the melted cooking chocolate. Fold the egg yolk cream gently into the egg whites in three batches, alternating with the flour, until combined.

3 Transfer the batter to the prepared springform tin and level the top. Bake for 25 minutes, reduce the oven temperature to 170°C (340°F) and continue to bake for about another 35 minutes. Take the cake out of the oven and set aside to cool a little before removing from the tin. Leave to cool completely on a wire rack. Use a sharp knife to level the top of the cake and cut it in half horizontally.

4 Gently warm the jam until it softens. Spread about one-third of the jam over the top of the bottom cake half. Top with the other half and brush all over with the remaining jam.

5 For the icing, soak the gelatine in cold water. Meanwhile, coarsely chop the chocolate. Transfer to a saucepan with the cream and gently melt over low heat, stirring continuously. As soon as the chocolate has melted, whisk in the gelatine until it has fully dissolved. Be careful not to let the mixture get too hot. Remove from the heat and leave to cool briefly before pouring the icing all over the cake. Leave to set for at least 6 hours, preferably overnight.

SPEKULATIUS SPICE TARTLETS

MAKES 12 TARTLETS

For the bases:
1 cup (150 g) plain flour
¼ cup (25 g) ground almonds
1 pinch salt
2 tbsp sugar
1½ tbsp vanilla sugar
1 tsp ground cinnamon
1 pinch ground cloves
1 pinch ground cardamom
⅓ cup (85 g) cold butter

For the filling:
250 g (9 oz) quark (20% fat) or Greek-style yogurt
200 g (7 oz) thick sour cream
100 g (3½ oz) fine sugar
1½ tbsp vanilla sugar
1½ tbsp cornflour
1 tsp grated orange zest
1 tbsp orange juice
100 ml (3½ fl oz) single (pure) cream
1 egg
1 egg yolk

For the topping:
100 ml (3½ fl oz) single (pure) cream
1 tsp sugar
2 German spekulatius cookies (or ground cinnamon, for dusting)

1 To make the bases, combine the flour, ground almonds, salt, sugar, vanilla sugar and spices. Dice the butter and rub into the dry ingredients until it resembles coarse breadcrumbs. Gradually add about 2 tbsp cold water and knead until well combined. Shape the dough into a ball, cover with plastic wrap and chill for at least 30 minutes.

2 Preheat the oven to 180°C (350°F). Line a 12-hole muffin tin with paper cases. Divide the dough into 12 portions. Roll each portion into a ball, press flat and then press into the paper cases. Transfer to the oven and bake for about 10 minutes. Remove from the oven and reduce the oven temperature to 160°C (320°F).

3 Meanwhile, for the filling, whisk the quark and sour cream until smooth. Whisk in the sugar, vanilla sugar and cornflour. Stir in the orange zest and juice, then quickly whisk in the cream, egg and egg yolk until everything is well combined. Divide the filling among the tartlet shells, using about 2–3 tablespoons in each, to come up to the edges of the paper cases.

4 Bake the tartlets for 20–24 minutes, then leave inside the closed oven to cool for about 15 minutes. Remove from the oven and set aside to cool completely.

5 For the topping, whip the cream and sugar until stiff, then spoon or pipe onto the cooled tartlets. Garnish with crumbled spekulatius cookies or ground cinnamon.

ORANGE AND PISTACHIO KUGELHOPF

MAKES ONE 25 CM (10 INCH) CAKE

250 g (1 cup) butter, softened
230 g (8 oz) sugar
¼ cup (55 g) vanilla sugar
5 eggs
320 g (11¼ oz) plain flour
½ cup (50 g) blanched, ground almonds
2½ tsp baking powder
1 pinch salt
100 ml (3½ fl oz) buttermilk
100 ml (3½ fl oz) orange juice
1 tbsp grated orange zest
⅓ cup (50 g) pistachios, chopped

For the topping:
150 g (5½ oz) icing (confectioners') sugar
2 tbsp orange juice
1–2 tsp grated orange zest
Chopped pistachios, for sprinkling

Also:
Butter, for greasing
Flour, for dusting

1 Preheat the oven to 180°C (350°F). Butter a kugelhopf tin and dust the tin with flour. Invert the tin and tap lightly to get rid of excess flour.

2 Combine the butter, sugar and vanilla sugar and whisk until creamy. Gradually add the eggs and continue to whisk until thick and foamy. Combine the flour, ground almonds, baking powder and salt in a separate bowl. Whisk together the buttermilk, orange juice and orange zest. Stir the orange and buttermilk mixture and the dry ingredients into the egg mixture, alternating between the two. Fold in the pistachios.

3 Transfer the batter to the tin and level the top. Bake for about 50–55 minutes. Use a toothpick to test for doneness (see page 10). Remove the cake from the oven and set aside to cool completely inside the tin. Once cool, invert and transfer to a serving plate.

4 For the topping, whisk together the icing sugar, orange juice and orange zest to make a thick icing. Pour the icing over the cooled cake. Sprinkle with the chopped pistachios to garnish.

BLACK FOREST CHERRY TRIFLES

MAKES 4–6

3 eggs
⅓ cup (70 g) sugar
⅓ cup (50 g) plain flour
1½ tbsp cornflour
2 tbsp cocoa powder

For the filling:
2 cups (320 g) fresh cherries, pitted (or drained morello cherries from a jar)
2 tbsp lemon juice
⅓ cup (80 g) jam-setting sugar (3:1)
2 tsp grated lemon zest
80 g (2¾ oz) milk chocolate
40 g (1½ oz) dark chocolate
3 egg yolks
1½ tbsp caster sugar
¼ cup (30 g) cornflour
325 ml (11 fl oz) milk
300 ml (10½ fl oz) single (pure) cream
Seeds of 1 vanilla bean
1 tbsp icing (confectioners') sugar

Also:
Butter, for greasing
Kirsch brandy, for drizzling
Fresh or morello cherries, for garnish

1 Preheat the oven to 180°C (350°F). Butter a 22 cm (8½ inch) springform tin.

2 Whisk the eggs and sugar until thick and foamy. Combine the flour, cornflour and cocoa powder and gently fold into the egg mixture. Spoon the batter into the prepared tin, smooth the top and bake for about 24 minutes. Remove the cake from the oven and leave it to cool in the tin before inverting it onto a wire rack to cool completely.

3 For the filling, blend the cherries and lemon juice, then strain into a small saucepan through a fine sieve. Stir in the jam-setting sugar and bring to the boil. Boil vigorously for about 5 minutes, stirring continuously. Add the lemon zest, remove from the heat, cover and leave to cool and set.

4 Chop both types of chocolate. Add the egg yolks, sugar, cornflour and milk to a saucepan and whisk until smooth. Place the pan over medium heat and simmer until the mixture thickens, stirring continuously. Remove from the heat and stir in the chopped chocolate to melt. Set aside to cool. Whip the cream with the vanilla seeds and icing sugar until stiff.

5 Halve the cooled sponge horizontally and cut out 8–12 discs to fit 4–6 dessert glasses. Place a sponge disc into each glass, drizzle with kirsch brandy and spread with the cherry jelly. Top with a layer of chocolate cream and another of vanilla cream. Repeat, starting with another piece of sponge per glass. Garnish the top cream layer with fresh cherries or morello cherries and a little cherry jelly. Refrigerate until serving.

BLUEBERRY CREAM PIE

MAKES ONE 20 CM (8 INCH) PIE

2 large eggs, separated
125 g (4½ oz) sugar
1½ tbsp vanilla sugar
2½ tbsp warm water
1 tbsp butter
⅔ cup (100 g) plain flour
3 tsp cocoa powder
½ tsp baking powder
1 pinch salt

For the blueberry cream:
4 gelatine sheets
150 g (5½ oz) low-fat quark or Greek-style yogurt
100 g (3½ oz) crème fraîche
⅓ cup (75 g) sugar
½ cup (120 ml) blueberry juice
200 ml (7 fl oz) single (pure) cream

For decorating:
100 ml (3½ fl oz) single (pure) cream
1½ tbsp vanilla sugar
1 tsp grated lemon zest
1¼ cups (200 g) blueberries

Also:
Butter, for greasing
Flour, for dusting

1 Preheat the oven to 190°C (375°F). Butter a 20 cm (8 inch) springform tin and dust with flour. Line the base of the tin with baking paper.

2 Whisk the egg yolks, sugar, vanilla sugar and warm water until thick and foamy, about 8 minutes. Melt the butter and leave to cool a little before stirring into the batter. Combine the flour, cocoa powder, baking powder and salt. Sift the mixture over the wet ingredients and fold in quickly. Beat the egg whites until stiff and gently fold in. Transfer the batter to the tin and bake for 20–25 minutes. Leave to cool briefly, then remove from the tin and set aside to cool completely on a wire rack. Transfer the sponge onto a serving plate.

3 For the cream, soak the gelatine in cold water for 5 minutes. Whisk the quark, crème fraîche, sugar and blueberry juice until smooth. Transfer the gelatine to a small saucepan over low heat and dissolve, stirring continuously. Be careful not to overheat it. Stir 2 tbsp of the quark mixture into the gelatine, then add the gelatine mixture to the remaining quark and mix to combine. Set the blueberry cream aside for about 30 minutes until it starts to set. Whip the cream until stiff, then fold it into the blueberry cream mixture. Place a cake ring around the sponge. Spread the blueberry cream over the sponge and refrigerate to set for at least 3 hours, preferably overnight.

4 For the decoration, whip the cream until stiff with the vanilla sugar and lemon zest. Spread on top of the cake. Gently pick through and wash the blueberries and pat dry. Arrange on top of the cake. Remove the cake ring and spread the cream mixture around the side of the cake. Refrigerate until serving.

PLUM JAM DOUGHNUTS

MAKES ABOUT 9

For the dough:
1⅔ cups (255 g) plain flour, plus extra, if needed
1½ tbsp sugar
1½ tbsp vanilla sugar
15 g (½ oz) fresh yeast
⅓ cup (75 ml) lukewarm milk
50 g (1¾ oz) butter
1 egg
1 egg yolk
1 pinch salt

For the plum jam:
600 g (1 lb 5 oz) ripe plums
1½ tbsp vanilla sugar
1–2 tbsp orange juice
120 g (4¼ oz) brown sugar
¼ tsp ground cinnamon
1–2 tsp Amaretto

Also:
Vegetable oil, for deep-frying (see page 9)
Caster sugar, for coating

1 Prepare the plum jam the day before, if possible. Wash and quarter the plums, removing the stones. Transfer the plums to an ovenproof saucepan together with the vanilla sugar and orange juice. Bring to the boil. Cover and simmer for about 10 minutes over low heat, stirring occasionally to prevent the plums from burning. Meanwhile, preheat the oven to 150°C (300°F). Blend the plums with a stick blender. Stir in one-third of the brown sugar and the cinnamon and place the saucepan into the oven. Cook the plums for about 30 minutes. Use a wooden spoon to keep the oven door ajar to allow moisture to escape. Remove from the oven, stir in half of the remaining sugar and cook for another 30 minutes. Add the remaining sugar and return the saucepan to the oven for a final 30 minutes. The plum jam should be beautifully smooth and thick. If necessary, return it to the oven for a little longer. Stir in the Amaretto and transfer the plum jam to a sterilised jar. This recipe will make about 250 g (9 oz).

2 For the dough, combine the flour, sugar and vanilla sugar in a mixing bowl. Make a well in the centre. Crumble the yeast and dissolve in the lukewarm milk. Pour the mixture into the well and gently stir, gradually incorporating the flour. Cover the bowl with plastic wrap and leave until the mixture develops bubbles, about 20 minutes.

3 Meanwhile, melt the butter and leave to cool a little. Add the butter, egg, egg yolk and salt to the yeast mixture and knead until well combined, about 5 minutes. Cover again and leave the dough to rise for 1 hour. Line a baking tray with baking paper. Shape the dough into nine balls, about 50 g (1¾ oz) each. Transfer the balls onto the baking tray, cover and leave to rise for another 20 minutes.

4 Pour enough oil into a saucepan or deep-fryer to allow the doughnuts to float as they are cooked. Heat the oil to about 170°C (338°F). Deep-fry the doughnuts in batches, cooking two or three at a time. Cook for 2–3 minutes, then turn and cook until golden brown all over. Transfer to a plate lined with paper towel to cool.

5 Transfer the plum jam to a piping bag fitted with a long, pointed nozzle. Pipe a little jam inside each cooled doughnut. Pour a generous amount of caster sugar into a bowl and turn the doughnuts in the sugar.

CHERRY YOGURT PIE

MAKES ONE 24 CM (9½ INCH) PIE

3 eggs, separated
1 pinch salt
100 g (3½ oz) sugar
2 tbsp Amaretto
140 g (5 oz) plain flour
1 tsp baking powder

For the filling:
8 gelatine sheets
500 g (1 lb 2 oz) plain yogurt (3.5% fat)
150 g (5½ oz) crème fraîche
100 g (3½ oz) sugar
Seeds of 1 vanilla bean
Grated zest of 1 lemon
1 cup (250 ml) single (pure) cream
¼ cup (85 g) cherry jam
1½ cups (300 g) bottled morello cherries, drained

Also:
Butter, for greasing
30 g (1 oz) amaretti biscuits

1 Preheat the oven to 190°C (375°F). Line the base of a springform tin with baking paper. Lightly butter the side of the tin. Beat the egg whites and salt until stiff. Whisk the egg yolks and sugar until foamy and stir in the Amaretto. Do not overmix. Combine the flour and baking powder and gently stir into the egg yolk mixture along with a third of the beaten egg whites. Carefully fold in the remaining egg whites.

2 Transfer the batter to the tin and level the top. Bake until golden brown, about 18–20 minutes. Leave to cool briefly, then remove from the tin and leave to cool completely on a wire rack. Transfer the sponge base to a serving plate and place a cake ring around it.

3 For the filling, briefly soak the gelatine in cold water. Whisk the yogurt and crème fraîche with the sugar, vanilla seeds and lemon zest. Gently squeeze a little water from the gelatine. Transfer to a small saucepan and dissolve over low heat, stirring continuously. Be careful not to overheat the gelatine. Stir 2–3 tbsp of the yogurt mixture into the gelatine, then add the gelatine mixture to the remaining yogurt mixture and stir to combine. Refrigerate the filling for about 20 minutes. Meanwhile, whip the cream until stiff. Fold the whipped cream into the yogurt mixture as soon as it starts to set.

4 Spread 1½ tbsp of the cherry jam on top of the sponge. Top with the yogurt cream and level the top. Refrigerate the pie for about 20 minutes. Combine the remaining cherry jam with the cherries and spread the mixture over the top of the pie. Refrigerate again for at least 2½ hours.

5 Carefully slide a thin knife around the inside of the cake ring and remove the ring. Put the amaretti biscuits into a resealable plastic bag and coarsely crush with a rolling pin. Sprinkle the crushed biscuits over the pie just before serving.

MERINGUE CAKE

MAKES ONE 26 CM (10½ INCH) CAKE

½ cup (125 g) butter, softened
125 g (4½ oz) sugar
1½ tbsp vanilla sugar
4 egg yolks
1 cup (150 g) plain flour
2 tsp baking powder
2 tbsp milk

For the meringue:
4 egg whites
250 g (9 oz) sugar

For the filling:
¼ cup (25 g) cornflour
100 g (3½ oz) sugar
¼ cup (60 ml) lemon juice
400 ml (14 fl oz) single (pure) cream
2 tsp grated lemon zest

Also:
Butter, for greasing
⅓ cup (50 g) chopped almonds, for garnish

1 Preheat the oven to 160°C (320°F). Line the bases of two 26 cm (10½ inch) springform tins with baking paper. Lightly butter the sides.

2 Whisk the butter, sugar and vanilla sugar until foamy. Add the egg yolks one by one. Combine the flour and baking powder and stir in together with the milk. Divide the batter evenly between the two tins and level the tops.

3 For the meringue, whisk the egg whites until semi-stiff, then gradually add the sugar. Continue to whisk until very firm peaks form. Spoon half of the meringue mixture over the cake batter in each tin and sprinkle with the chopped almonds. Bake the cakes, one at a time, for about 35 minutes, until the meringue has colored nicely. Leave the cakes to cool completely, then slide a sharp knife around the edges and remove the cakes from the tins. This is best done by sliding two large, flat cake servers between the cake base and baking paper to lift the bases carefully. Transfer one base to a serving plate.

4 For the filling, pour ½ cup (125 ml) cold water into a saucepan and whisk in the cornflour to dissolve. Add the sugar and bring to the boil, then simmer until the mixture thickens. Stir in the lemon juice and transfer the mixture to a bowl. Leave to cool, stirring occasionally. Meanwhile, whip the cream until stiff. Stir in the lemon zest. Combine about a quarter of the cream with the lemon mixture, then gently fold in the remaining cream.

5 Spread the lemon cream evenly over the first sponge base. Carefully place the second base on top. This cake is best prepared a day ahead to give it time to develop its full flavor.

BAUMKUCHEN TRIANGLES

1 Thoroughly blend the milk with the marzipan and Amaretto. Whisk the butter and icing sugar until creamy. Whisk in the egg yolks one by one. Combine the marzipan mixture with the orange zest.

2 Whisk the egg whites and salt until stiff. Gradually add the sugar and vanilla sugar and continue to whisk until firm peaks form. Combine the flour, ground almonds and cornflour. Gently fold the dry ingredients into the egg whites, then fold this mixture into the marzipan mixture.

3 Preheat the oven to 250°C (500°F), using the grill function. Line the base of a springform tin with baking paper and butter the side. Spread 2 heaped tablespoons of the batter over the base of the tin. Transfer the tin to the hot oven and bake until golden brown, about 3–4 minutes. Spread another 2 tablespoons of the batter on top and bake. Continue until you have used up all the batter, making about 8–10 layers.

4 Remove the cake from the tin and leave to cool. Slice into lengths about 2.5 cm (1 inch) wide and cut these into triangles. Melt both types of chocolate together with the oil. Glaze the cake triangles with the chocolate mixture. Leave to cool on a cooling rack.

MAKES ABOUT 40 PIECES

2½ tbsp milk
125 g (4½ oz) marzipan paste, grated
1 tbsp Amaretto
175 g (6 oz) butter, softened
⅔ cup (80 g) icing (confectioners') sugar
5 eggs, separated
1 tsp grated orange zest
1 pinch salt
⅓ cup (80 g) sugar
1½ tbsp vanilla sugar
85 g (3 oz) plain flour
¼ cup (25 g) blanched, ground almonds
⅓ cup (40 g) cornflour

Also:
Butter, for greasing
100 g (3½ oz) dark chocolate
50 g (1¾ oz) milk chocolate
2 tsp coconut oil

MARBLED CHEESECAKE

MAKES ONE 24 CM (9½ INCH) CHEESECAKE

For the base:
75 g (2½ oz) butter
175 g (6 oz) digestive biscuits
1½ tsp brown sugar
1 generous pinch of salt

For the filling:
500 g (1 lb 2 oz) cream cheese
200 g (7 oz) low-fat quark or Greek-style yogurt
185 g (6½ oz) caster sugar
1½ tbsp vanilla sugar
¼ cup (30 g) cornflour
1½ tsp grated lemon zest
1 tbsp lemon juice
⅔ cup (175 ml) single (pure) cream
2 eggs
1 egg yolk

Also:
Butter, for greasing
About 2 cups (250 g) mixed fresh or frozen berries, thawed
1 tsp cornflour
About 1 tbsp honey

1 Preheat the oven to 180°C (350°F). Carefully line a 24 cm (9½ inch) springform tin with baking paper and butter the side.

2 For the base, melt the butter in a small saucepan. Put the biscuits in a resealable plastic bag and finely crush with a rolling pin. Thoroughly combine the biscuit crumbs with the melted butter, brown sugar and salt. Press the biscuit mixture into the tin evenly and firmly and bake for 8–10 minutes. Set aside to cool. Reduce the oven to 160°C (320°F).

3 Blend the berries and strain them through a fine sieve. Remove about 2 tablespoons for marbling and refrigerate the rest for the sauce.

4 For the filling, mix the cream cheese and quark together until smooth. Whisk in the sugar, vanilla sugar and cornflour. Stir in the lemon zest and juice, then quickly whisk in the cream, eggs and egg yolk, mixing until everything is well combined. Do not overmix to prevent bubbles from forming when baking. Spread the filling evenly over the base. Dot the top with the 2 tablespoons blended berries. Pull a fork through the berries to create a marbled effect.

5 Bake the cheesecake for about 45 minutes. Do not open the oven door during cooking, or the surface will crack. When the cheesecake is cooked, switch off the oven and leave the cake to cool. Leave the oven door closed for the first 30 minutes, then open the door slightly and leave to cool for another 1½ hours. Remove the cheesecake from the oven, set aside to cool completely, then refrigerate for at least 6 hours.

6 Before serving, carefully slide a sharp knife around the cake edge. Remove the cheesecake from the tin and transfer to a serving plate. Bring the remaining strained berries to the boil in a small saucepan. Dissolve the cornflour in a little cold water. Whisk into the fruit and simmer for 1–2 minutes, stirring, to thicken. Sweeten with honey. Serve the berry coulis with the cheesecake.

MINI APPLE AND CINNAMON SCROLLS

MAKES 12

1½ cups (225 g) plain flour
1 pinch salt
2 tbsp caster sugar
10 g (¼ oz) fresh yeast
⅓ cup (80 ml) lukewarm milk
1 tbsp butter, melted
1 egg

For the filling:
1–2 small apples, such as granny smith or braeburn
2 tbsp chopped hazelnuts
1 tbsp lemon juice
Seeds from ½ vanilla bean
1½ tbsp butter, plus 1 tbsp extra
1 heaped tbsp honey
2 tbsp caster sugar
2 tsp ground cinnamon

For the glaze:
⅔ cup (85 g) icing (confectioners') sugar
About ¼ cup (60 ml) apple juice

Also:
Butter, for greasing
Flour, for dusting
Milk, for brushing

1 Combine the flour, salt and sugar in a mixing bowl. Crumble the yeast and dissolve in the lukewarm milk. Add the yeast milk, the cooled, melted butter and the egg to the flour mixture and knead everything together to make a smooth dough. Cover the bowl with plastic wrap and leave the dough to rise in a warm place for about 2 hours.

2 Meanwhile, peel, core and very finely dice the apples for the filling. Combine with the nuts, lemon juice and vanilla seeds. Heat the 1 tablespoon of butter in a frying pan. Add the apple mixture and cook for about 8 minutes. Stir in the honey and continue to cook until lightly caramelised, about 2 minutes. Remove the pan from the heat. Combine the sugar and cinnamon in a small bowl. Melt the 1½ tablespoons of butter.

3 Butter a 12-hole muffin tin and dust with flour. Alternatively, line the muffin holes with paper cases to make it easier to remove the scrolls. Dust your work surface with flour and roll the dough out to a thin rectangle about 20 x 36 cm (8 x 14¼ inches) in size and 3 mm (⅛ inch) thick. Generously spread the melted butter over the dough, all the way to the edges. Sprinkle the cinnamon sugar evenly over the butter, leaving a little margin along the top, long edge. Spread the apple mixture across and press in gently. Roll the dough up from the long side closest to you and cut the roll into 12 even slices. Transfer the slices to the prepared muffin tin. Cover with plastic wrap and leave to rise for another 15 minutes.

4 Preheat the oven to 190°C (375°F). Brush the cinnamon scrolls with a little milk and bake until golden brown, about 15 minutes. Leave to cool to lukewarm before removing the scrolls carefully from the tins. Carefully slide a thin, sharp knife around the edges of the muffin holes and gently lift out the scrolls.

5 For the glaze, whisk the icing sugar into the apple juice and drizzle or spread over the cinnamon scrolls.

SWEET BERRY COBBLER

SERVES 4

About 350 g (12 oz) mixed fresh berries (or frozen berries, thawed and drained)
3 ripe nectarines or peaches
1 cup (250 ml) blackcurrant juice
2 tbsp lemon juice
⅓ cup (75 g) sugar
1½ tbsp vanilla sugar
3 heaped tsp cornflour

For the dough:
1⅓ cups (200 g) plain flour
¼ cup (50 g) sugar
1½ tbsp vanilla sugar
1 tbsp baking powder
1 pinch salt
Grated zest of 1 lemon
1 tsp ground cinnamon
100 g (3½ oz) cold butter
1 egg
2 tbsp crème fraîche
About ⅓ cup (80 ml) milk

Also:
Icing (confectioners') sugar, for dusting
Vanilla custard, to serve

1 Pick through the berries, rinse gently and drain. If using strawberries, quarter any large berries and halve any smaller ones. Wash and pat dry the nectarines or peaches. Remove the stones and dice finely.

2 Bring the blackcurrant juice, lemon juice, sugar and vanilla sugar to the boil in a small saucepan. Simmer over low heat for about 10 minutes to reduce. Dissolve the cornflour in a little cold water. Whisk into the juice mixture and simmer, stirring, to bind. Stir in the fruit as soon as the liquid starts to thicken. Remove from the heat and leave to cool. If the mixture is still too runny, remove the fruit with a slotted spoon and transfer to an 800 ml (28 fl oz) ovenproof dish. The fruit should only come halfway up the side of the dish.

3 Preheat the oven to 180°C (350°F). For the dough, combine the flour, sugar, vanilla sugar, baking powder, salt, lemon zest and cinnamon in a mixing bowl. Dice the butter and rub into the flour until the mixture resembles coarse breadcrumbs. Whisk the egg and crème fraîche together in a measuring jug and add enough milk to make ¾ cup (180 ml). Stir the egg mixture into the flour mixture. Use a tablespoon to scoop out even portions of the dough and place them on top of the fruit, leaving a little space in between.

4 Bake the cobbler for about 35 minutes until the dough has risen nicely and taken on a golden brown color. Leave to cool a little, dust with icing sugar and serve warm with custard.

MINI MARBLED KUGELHOPFS

MAKES 12

½ cup (125 g) butter, softened
100 g (3½ oz) sugar
1½ tbsp vanilla sugar
3 eggs
1½ cups (225 g) plain flour
1½ tsp baking powder
1 pinch salt
100 ml (3½ fl oz) buttermilk
3 tsp cocoa powder
40 g (1½ oz) dark chocolate

Also:
Butter, for greasing
Flour, for dusting
Icing (confectioners') sugar, for dusting

1 Preheat the oven to 180°C (350°F). Butter a 12-hole mini kugelhopf tin and dust with flour. Invert and tap lightly to get rid of excess flour.

2 Combine the butter, sugar and vanilla sugar and whisk until creamy. Stir in the eggs one by one. Combine the flour, baking powder and salt in a separate bowl. Add the dry ingredients and three-quarters of the buttermilk to the egg mixture in batches, alternating between the two. Do not overmix. Remove a generous third of the batter and combine with the remaining buttermilk and cocoa powder. Very finely chop the chocolate and mix into the cocoa batter.

3 Transfer the light batter to a piping bag and pipe into the prepared tin. Transfer the dark batter to another piping bag and pipe on top. The moulds should not be filled to the top, as the batter will rise. Pull a fork through the two batters to create a marbled effect.

4 Bake the mini kugelhopfs for 17–20 minutes. Use a toothpick to test for doneness (see page 10). Leave to cool completely and dust with icing sugar to serve.

Hansel and Gretel

SWEET AND SCRUMPTIOUS

Beside a great forest dwelt a poor wood-cutter...

...with his wife and two children. The boy was called Hansel and the girl, Gretel. He had little to bite and to break, and once when great dearth fell on the land, he could no longer procure even daily bread. Now when he thought over this by night in his bed, and tossed about in his anxiety, he groaned and said to his wife: 'What is to become of us? How are we to feed our poor children, when we no longer have anything even for ourselves?' 'I'll tell you what, husband,' answered the woman, 'early tomorrow morning we will take the children out into the forest to where it is the thickest; there we will light a fire for them, and give each of them one more piece of bread, and then we will go to our work and leave them alone. They will not find the way home again, and we shall be rid of them.' 'No, wife,' said the man, 'I will not do that; how can I bear to leave my children alone in the forest? The wild animals would soon come and tear them to pieces.' 'O, you fool!' said she, 'then we must all four die of hunger; you may as well plane the planks for our coffins.' And she left him no peace until he consented. 'But I feel very sorry for the poor children, all the same,' said the man.

The two children had also not been able to sleep for hunger, and had heard what their stepmother had said to their father. Gretel wept bitter tears, and said to Hansel: 'Now all is over with us.' 'Be quiet, Gretel,' said Hansel, 'do not distress yourself, I will soon find a way to help us.' And when the old folks had fallen asleep, he got up, put on his little coat, opened the door below, and crept outside. The moon shone brightly, and the white pebbles that lay in front of the house glittered like real silver pennies. Hansel stooped and stuffed the little pocket of his coat with as many as he could get in. Then he went back and said to Gretel: 'Be comforted, dear little sister, and sleep in peace, God will not forsake us,' and he lay down again in his bed. When day dawned, but before the sun had risen, the woman came and awoke the two children, saying: 'Get up, you sluggards! We are going into the forest to fetch wood.' She gave each a little piece of bread, and said: 'There is something for your dinner, but do not eat it up before then, for you will get nothing else.' Gretel took the bread under her apron, as Hansel had the pebbles in his pocket. Then they all set out together on the way to the forest. When they had walked a short time, Hansel stood still and peeped back at the house, and did so again and again. His father said: 'Hansel, what are you looking at there and staying behind for? Pay attention, and do not forget how to use your legs.' 'Ah, father,' said Hansel, 'I am looking at my little white cat, which is sitting up on the roof, and wants to say goodbye to me.' The wife said: 'Fool, that is not your little cat, that is the morning sun that is shining on the chimneys.' Hansel, however, had not been looking back at the cat, but had been constantly throwing one of the white pebble-stones out of his pocket on the road.

When they had reached the middle of the forest, the father said: 'Now, children, pile up some wood, and I will light a fire that you may not be cold.' Hansel and Gretel gathered brushwood together, as high as a little hill. It was lighted, and when the flames were burning very high, the woman said: 'Now, children, lay yourselves down by the fire and rest, we will go into the forest and cut some wood. When we have done, we will come back and fetch you.'

Hansel and Gretel sat by the fire, and when noon came, each ate a little piece of bread, and as they heard the strokes of the wood-axe they believed that their father was near. It was not the axe, however, but a branch that he had fastened to a withered tree, which the wind was blowing backwards and forwards. And as they had been sitting such a long time, their eyes closed with fatigue, and they fell fast asleep. When at last they awoke, it was already dark night. Gretel began to cry and said: 'How are we to get out of the forest now?' But Hansel comforted her and said: 'Just wait a little, until the moon has risen, and then we will soon find the way.' And when the full moon had risen, Hansel took his little sister by the hand, and followed the pebbles that shone like newly coined silver pieces, and showed them the way.

They walked the whole night long, and by break of day came once more to their father's house. They knocked at the door, and when the woman opened it and saw that it was Hansel and Gretel, she said: 'You naughty children, why have you slept so long in the forest? We thought you were never coming back at all!' The father, however, rejoiced, for it had cut him to the heart to leave them behind alone.

Not long afterwards, there was once more great dearth throughout the land, and the children heard their mother saying at night to their father: 'Everything is eaten again, we have one half loaf left, and that is the end. The children must go, we will take them farther into the wood, so that they will not find their way out again; there is no other means of saving ourselves!' The man's heart was heavy, and he thought: 'It would be better for you to share the last mouthful with your children.' The woman, however, would listen to nothing that he had to say, but scolded and reproached him, and as he had yielded the first time, he had to do so a second time also.

The children were still awake and had heard the conversation. When the old folks were asleep, Hansel again got up, and wanted to go out and pick up pebbles as he had done before, but the woman had locked the door, and Hansel could not get out. Nevertheless he comforted his little sister, and said: 'Do not cry, Gretel. Go to sleep quietly; the good God will help us.'

Early in the morning came the woman, and took the children out of their beds. Their piece of bread was given to them, but it was still smaller than the time before. On the way into the forest Hansel crumbled his in his pocket, and often stood still and threw a morsel on the ground. 'Hansel, why do you stop and look round?' said the father. 'I am looking back at my little pigeon, which is sitting on the roof, and wants to say goodbye to me,' answered Hansel. 'Fool!' said the woman, 'that is not your little pigeon, that is the morning sun that is shining on the chimney.' However Hansel, little by little, threw all the crumbs on the path.

The woman led the children still deeper into the forest, where they had never in their lives been before. Then a great fire was again made, and the mother said: 'Just sit there, you children, and when you are tired you may sleep a little; we are going into the forest to cut wood, and in the evening when we are done, we will come and fetch you.' When it was noon, Gretel shared her piece of bread with Hansel, who had scattered his by the way. Then they fell asleep and evening passed, but no one came to the poor children. They did not awake until it was dark night, and Hansel comforted his little sister and said: 'Just wait, Gretel, until the moon rises, and then we shall see the crumbs of bread that I have strewn about; they will show us our way home again.' When the moon came they set out, but they found no crumbs, for the many thousands of birds that fly about in the woods and fields had picked them all up. Hansel said to Gretel: 'We shall soon find the way,' but they did not find it. They walked the whole night and all the next day from morning till evening, but they did not get out of the forest, and were very hungry, for they had nothing to eat but two or three berries, which grew on the ground. As they were so weary that their legs would carry them no longer, they lay down beneath a tree and fell asleep.

'DO NOT CRY, GRETEL. GO TO SLEEP QUIETLY. THE GOOD GOD WILL HELP US.'

It was now three mornings since they had left their father's house. They began to walk again, but they always came deeper into the forest, and if help did not come soon, they must die of hunger and weariness. When it was mid-day, they saw a beautiful snow-white bird sitting on a bough, which sang so delightfully that they stood still and listened to it. And when its song was over, it spread its wings and flew away before them, and they followed it until they reached a little house, on the roof of which it alighted; and when they approached the little house they saw that it was built of bread and covered with cakes, but that the windows were of clear sugar. 'We will set to work on that,' said Hansel, 'and have a good meal. I will eat a bit of the roof, and you Gretel, can eat some of the window; it will taste sweet.' Hansel reached up above, and broke off a little of the roof to try how it tasted, and Gretel leant against the window and nibbled at the panes. Then a soft voice cried from the parlour:

'Nibble, nibble, gnaw.
Who is nibbling at my little house?'

The children answered:

'The wind, the wind,
The heaven-born wind,'

And they went on eating. Hansel, who liked the taste of the roof, tore down a great piece of it, and Gretel pushed out the whole of one round window-pane, sat down and enjoyed it. Suddenly the door opened, and a woman as old as the hills, who supported herself on crutches, came creeping out. Hansel and Gretel were so terribly frightened that they let fall what they had in their hands. The old woman, however, nodded her head, and said: 'Oh, you dear children, who has brought you here? Do come in, and stay with me. No harm shall happen to you.' She took them both by the hand, and led them into her little house. Then good food was set before them, milk and pancakes, with sugar, apples and nuts. Afterwards two pretty little beds were covered with clean white linen, and Hansel and Gretel lay down in them, and thought they were in heaven.

The old woman had only pretended to be so kind; she was in reality a wicked witch, who lay in wait for children, and had only built the little house of bread in order to entice them there. When a child fell into her power, she killed it, cooked and ate it. Witches have red eyes, and cannot see far, but they have a keen scent like the beasts, and are aware when human beings draw near. When Hansel and Gretel came into her neighbourhood, she laughed with malice, and said mockingly: 'I have them, they shall not escape me again!'

Early in the morning before the children were awake, she was already up, and when she saw both of them sleeping and looking so pretty, with their plump and rosy cheeks, she muttered to herself: 'That will be a dainty mouthful!' Then she seized Hansel with her shrivelled hand, carried him into a little stable, and locked him in behind a grated door. Scream as he might, it would not help him. Then she went to Gretel, shook her till she awoke, and cried: 'Get up, lazy thing, fetch some water, and cook something good for your brother. He is in the stable outside, and is to be made fat. When he is fat, I will eat him.' Gretel began to weep bitterly, but it was all in vain, for she was forced to do what the wicked witch commanded.

'WHO IS NIBBLING AT MY LITTLE HOUSE?'

And now the best food was cooked for poor Hansel, but Gretel got nothing but crab-shells. Every morning the woman crept to the little stable, and cried: 'Hansel, stretch out your finger that I may feel if you will soon be fat.' Hansel, however, stretched out a little bone to her, and the old woman, who had dim eyes, thought it was Hansel's finger, and was astonished that there was no way of fattening him. When four weeks had gone by, and Hansel still remained thin, she was seized with impatience and would not wait any longer. 'Now, then, Gretel,' she cried to the girl, 'stir yourself, and bring some water. Let Hansel be fat or lean, tomorrow I will kill him, and cook him.' Ah, how the poor little sister did lament when she had to fetch the water, and how her tears did flow down her cheeks! 'Dear God, do help us,' she cried. 'If the wild beasts in the forest had but devoured us, we should at any rate have died together.' 'Just keep your noise to yourself,' said the old woman, 'it won't help you at all.'

Early in the morning, Gretel had to go out and hang up the cauldron with the water, and light the fire. 'We will bake first,' said the old woman. 'I have already heated the oven, and kneaded the dough.' She pushed poor Gretel out to the oven, from which flames of fire were already darting. 'Creep in,' said the witch, 'and see if it is properly heated, so that we can put the bread in.' And once Gretel was inside, the witch intended to shut the oven and let her bake in it, and then she would eat her, too. But Gretel saw what she had in mind, and said: 'I do not know how I am to do it; how do I get in?' 'Silly goose,' said the old woman. 'The door is big enough; just look, I can get in myself!' and she crept up and thrust her head into the oven. Then Gretel gave her a push that drove her far inside, and shut the iron door, and fastened the bolt. The witch began to howl quite horribly, but Gretel ran away and the godless witch was miserably burnt to death.

Gretel, however, ran like lightning to Hansel, opened his little stable, and cried: 'Hansel, we are saved! The old witch is dead!' Then Hansel sprang like a bird from its cage when the door is opened. How they did rejoice and embrace each other, and dance about and kiss each other! And as they had no longer any need to fear her, they went into the witch's house, and in every corner there stood chests full of pearls and jewels. 'These are far better than pebbles!' said Hansel, and thrust into his pockets whatever could be got in, and Gretel said: 'I, too, will take something home with me,' and filled her pinafore full. 'But now we must be off,' said Hansel, 'that we may get out of the witch's forest.'

When they had walked for two hours, they came to a great stretch of water. 'We cannot cross,' said Hansel, 'I see no foot-plank, and no bridge.' 'And there is also no ferry,' answered Gretel, 'but a white duck is swimming there: if I ask her, she will help us over.' Then she cried:

'Little duck, little duck, dost thou see,
Hansel and Gretel are waiting for thee?
There's never a plank, or bridge in sight,
Take us across on thy back so white.'

The duck came to them, and Hansel seated himself on its back, and told his sister to sit by him. 'No,' replied Gretel, 'that will be too heavy for the little duck; she shall take us across, one after the other.' The good little duck did so, and when they were once safely across and had walked for a short time, the forest seemed to be more and more familiar to them, and at length they saw from afar their father's house. Then they began to run, rushed into the parlour, and threw themselves round their father's neck. The man had not known one happy hour since he had left the children in the forest; the woman, however, was dead. Gretel emptied her pinafore until pearls and precious stones ran about the room, and Hansel threw one handful after another out of his pocket to add to them. Then all anxiety was at an end, and they lived together in perfect happiness. My tale is done, there runs a mouse; whosoever catches it, may make himself a big fur cap out of it.

BLACKCURRANT MERINGUE COOKIES

MAKES ABOUT 25

120 g (4¼ oz) plain flour
⅓ cup (40 g) blanched, ground almonds
1½ tablespoons sugar
1½ tbsp vanilla sugar
1 pinch ground cinnamon
1 pinch salt
100 g (3½ oz) cold butter
1 large egg yolk
1 tbsp cocoa powder

For the meringue:
1 large egg white
½ cup (60 g) icing (confectioners') sugar

Also:
Flour, for dusting
About 200 g (7 oz) blackcurrant jelly

1 Combine the flour, ground almonds, sugar, vanilla sugar, cinnamon and salt in a mixing bowl. Dice the butter and rub into the flour until the mixture resembles coarse breadcrumbs. Add the egg yolk and knead to combine well. Divide the dough into two equal portions. Add the cocoa to one half and combine thoroughly. Shape the dough portions into balls, cover with plastic wrap and chill for 40 minutes.

2 Roll out one ball of dough about 3 mm (⅛ inch) thick on a lightly floured surface and use a 2.5 cm (1 inch) cookie cutter to cut out small discs. Repeat with the second ball of dough. Line two baking trays with baking paper and divide the discs among them, sorted by color and leaving a little space between.

3 Preheat the oven to 180°C (350°F). For the meringue, whisk the egg white until stiff, gradually adding the icing sugar. Transfer the mixture to a piping bag fitted with a fluted nozzle and pipe small mounds on top of all the white dough discs. Place the tray with the meringue topping into the oven and bake for 14–18 minutes. Remove from the oven and leave the cookies to cool completely. Next, place the tray with the dark discs into the oven and bake for 10–12 minutes.

4 Bring the blackcurrant jelly to the boil in a small saucepan. Reduce the heat and simmer briefly. Stir until smooth, then set aside to cool. Spread each dark cookie with a little jelly. Top with a meringue-topped cookie and gently press together. Leave the cookies to dry.

BANANA AND PECAN NUT CAKE

1 Preheat the oven to 180°C (350°F). Butter a 25 cm (10 inch) loaf tin and dust with flour. Invert and tap lightly to get rid of excess flour.

2 Finely mash the bananas with a fork. Whisk the butter and sugar until creamy, then gradually incorporate the eggs. Mix in the mashed banana and coconut milk. Combine the flour, ground hazelnuts, baking powder and salt and quickly stir into the wet mixture. Fold in the chopped pecans and transfer the batter to the tin. Level the top.

3 Bake the cake for about 60–70 minutes. Use a toothpick to test for doneness (see page 10). Remove from the oven and set aside to cool completely. Increase the oven to 200°C (400°F) and line a baking tray with baking paper.

4 For the topping, melt the chocolate, stirring continuously, in a bowl set over a saucepan of simmering water. Combine the sugar and boiling water in a bowl. Add the chopped nuts and toss. Transfer the nuts to the baking tray in a single layer and roast in the oven for about 10 minutes, turning once. Finely chop the banana chips and combine with the shredded coconut. Remove the cooled cake from its tin and place onto a serving plate. Pour the chocolate mixture over the cake. Sprinkle with the toasted nuts, chopped banana chips and grated coconut.

MAKES ONE 25 CM (10 INCH) LOAF

3 very ripe bananas, about 350 g (12 oz) peeled
150 g (5½ oz) butter, softened
185 g (6½ oz) sugar
3 eggs
100 ml (3½ fl oz) coconut milk
280 g (10 oz) plain flour
½ cup (50 g) ground hazelnuts
1 tsp baking powder
¼ tsp salt
1 cup (100 g) pecan nuts, finely chopped

Also:

Butter, for greasing
Flour, for dusting
150 g (5½ oz) milk cooking chocolate
1–2 tsp sugar
1½ tbsp boiling water
½ cup (50 g) pecan nuts, coarsely chopped
1 handful banana chips
2 tsp shredded coconut

PEAR AND CRANBERRY GALETTE

MAKES 1 GALETTE

1½ cups (220 g) plain flour
¼ cup (30 g) cornflour
2 tsp sugar
1 pinch salt
½ cup (125 g) cold butter
50 g (1¾ oz) crème fraîche
⅓ cup (75 ml) iced water

For the filling:
4 pears
Juice of ½ small lemon
¼ cup (60 g) sugar
1½ tbsp vanilla sugar
1 tbsp honey
½ tsp ground cinnamon
1 pinch ground cardamom
2 tbsp dried cranberries

Also:
Flour, for dusting
1 egg yolk, lightly beaten
1–2 tsp brown sugar
1 tbsp butter
1 handful flaked almonds

1 Combine the flour, cornflour, sugar and salt in a mixing bowl. Dice the butter and rub into the flour until the mixture resembles coarse breadcrumbs. Whisk the crème fraîche together with the iced water and add to the dough. Knead everything together. Shape the dough into a ball, cover with plastic wrap and chill for at least 30 minutes.

2 Meanwhile, prepare the filling. Peel the pears, remove the cores, slice thinly and drizzle with lemon juice. Whisk the sugar, vanilla sugar, honey, cinnamon and cardamom into ¼ cup (60 ml) water in a small saucepan and bring to the boil. Simmer briefly until the sugar has dissolved. Add the sliced pears and stew for about 4 minutes over low heat. Remove the fruit with a slotted spoon and boil the liquid over high heat for a few minutes to reduce. Be careful not to burn it. Pour the liquid over the fruit and stir in the cranberries.

3 Preheat the oven to 190°C (375°F). Line a baking tray with baking paper. Dust your work surface lightly with flour and roll out the dough to a circle about 30 cm (12 inches) in diameter and 4 mm (3⁄16 inch) thick. Spread the pear mixture on top, leaving a 4 cm (1½ inch) edge. Fold the edge over the filling on six sides (or whichever way you prefer). Brush with the egg yolk and sprinkle with brown sugar. Dot with the butter, sprinkle with the flaked almonds and bake until golden brown, about 35 minutes.

MATCHA AND VANILLA COOKIES

MAKES ABOUT 40

For the matcha dough:
1½ tsp good-quality matcha powder
⅔ cup (80 g) icing (confectioners') sugar
1 cup (150 g) plain flour, plus extra for kneading
60 g (2¼ oz) blanched, ground almonds
75 g (2½ oz) cold butter
1 small egg

For the vanilla dough:
1 cup (150 g) plain flour, plus extra for kneading
60 g (2¼ oz) blanched, ground almonds
⅔ cup (80 g) icing (confectioners') sugar
Seeds of 1 vanilla bean
1 pinch salt
75 g (2½ oz) cold butter
1 small egg

Also:
150 g (5½ oz) white cooking chocolate
Matcha powder, for dusting

1 For the matcha dough, thoroughly combine the matcha powder with the icing sugar. Stir in the flour and ground almonds. Dice the butter and rub into the flour mixture until the mixture resembles coarse breadcrumbs. Add the egg and knead everything until well combined. Add a little more flour if the dough seems too sticky. Halve the dough. Shape each half into a roll about 20 cm (8 inches) long, cover with plastic wrap and refrigerate for at least 1 hour. (Alternatively, freeze the dough for about 20 minutes.)

2 For the vanilla dough, combine the flour, ground almonds, icing sugar, vanilla seeds and salt. Dice the butter and rub into the flour mixture until the mixture resembles coarse breadcrumbs. Add the egg and knead everything until well combined. Add a little more flour if the dough seems too sticky. Halve the dough. Press each half gently to flatten, cover with plastic wrap and refrigerate for at least 1 hour. (Alternatively, freeze the dough for about 20 minutes.)

3 Roll out the vanilla dough to make two rectangles about 20 cm (8 inches) long and 5 mm (¼ inch) thick. Brush with a little water and place a matcha dough roll on top of each rectangle. Tightly fold the vanilla dough over the matcha rolls, press the edges together to seal and trim off the excess vanilla dough. Wrap the rolls in plastic wrap again and refrigerate for another 1½ hours. (Alternatively, freeze the dough rolls for about 30 minutes.)

4 Preheat the oven to 180°C (350°F) and line two baking trays with baking paper. Cut the dough rolls into 5 mm (¼ inch) slices and transfer these onto the baking trays. Bake for 10–12 minutes, one tray after the other. Remove from the oven and leave the cookies to cool on a wire rack. They will firm up as they cool.

5 Melt the cooking chocolate in a bowl sitting over a saucepan of simmering water. Leave to cool slightly, then dip the cookies halfway into the chocolate. Spread the cookies on a sheet of baking paper in a single layer, dust with a little matcha powder and leave to dry.

LINZER TARTLETS

MAKES 6

1⅓ cups (200 g) plain flour
125 g (4½ oz) ground hazelnuts
125 g (4½ oz) sugar
1 tsp ground cinnamon
1 pinch ground cloves
1 pinch ground cardamom
1 pinch ground allspice
1 tsp grated orange zest
150 g (5½ oz) cold butter
1 egg
¾ cup (250 g) raspberry jam

Also:
Butter, for greasing
Flour, for dusting
1 egg yolk, lightly beaten

1 Combine the flour, ground hazelnuts, sugar, spices and orange zest. Dice the butter and rub into the flour until the mixture resembles coarse breadcrumbs. Add the egg and knead everything until well combined. Shape the dough into a ball, cover with plastic wrap and chill for at least 30 minutes.

2 Preheat the oven to 180°C (350°F). Butter six 10 cm (4 inch) shallow tartlet tins and dust with flour. Invert the tins and tap lightly to get rid of excess flour.

3 Set aside about 200 g (7 oz) of the dough. Roll out the rest of the dough on a floured surface until it is about 3 mm (⅛ inch) thick. Cut out six discs to line the tins. Whisk the jam until smooth and spread it evenly over the bases.

4 Roll out the remaining dough until 3 mm (⅛ inch) thick. Cut into 5 mm (¼ inch) strips and arrange the strips on top of the jam in a lattice pattern. Brush the lattices and tartlet edges with the beaten egg yolk.

5 Bake the tartlets for about 30 minutes. Remove from the oven and leave to cool completely.

APPLE TARTE TATIN

MAKES ONE 22 CM (8½ INCH) TART

1 cup (150 g) plain flour
¼ cup (30 g) ground hazelnuts
2 tbsp sugar
1½ tbsp vanilla sugar
½ tsp ground cinnamon
¼ tsp ground cardamom
1 pinch salt
100 g (3½ oz) cold butter
1 egg

For the filling:
3–4 small apples
¼ cup (50 g) sugar
1 tbsp rum
⅓ cup (50 g) hazelnuts or walnuts, chopped
25 g (1 oz) butter
1 handful raisins

Also:
Flour, for dusting
Vanilla ice cream, to serve

1 Combine the flour, nuts, sugar, vanilla sugar, cinnamon, cardamom and salt in a mixing bowl. Dice the butter and toss through the flour mixture. Add the egg and knead everything together to make a soft shortcrust pastry dough. Refrigerate the dough for at least 30 minutes.

2 Meanwhile, peel and core the apples for the filling. Halve the apples horizontally. Caramelise the sugar with the rum and chopped nuts until lightly browned in a small ovenproof frying pan, about 22 cm (8½ inches). Remove the pan from the heat and stir in the butter. Be careful – it will foam up. Arrange the halved apples tightly in the pan, cut side up, and cook them in the caramel sauce over low to medium heat for about 10 minutes. Stuff the apples with a few raisins, then take the pan off the heat and set aside to cool.

3 Preheat the oven to 180°C (350°F). Roll out the dough on a lightly floured surface to make a disc large enough to cover the pan. Place the dough on top of the cooled apples, pushing the edges carefully down and around the apples. Prick the dough with a fork and bake until golden brown, about 35 minutes. Remove from the oven. Cover the pan with a serving plate and immediately invert the tart onto the plate. Be careful with the hot caramel sauce. Serve immediately with vanilla ice cream.

QUICK NUT CAKE

MAKES ONE 20 CM (8 INCH) CAKE

⅔ cup (75 g) walnuts
4 eggs, separated
½ cup (125 g) butter, softened
125 g (4½ oz) caster sugar
125 g (4½ oz) ground hazelnuts
125 g (4½ oz) quark (40% fat) or Greek-style yogurt
Seeds of ½ vanilla bean
¼ cup (60 ml) apple juice
½ tsp ground cinnamon
1 pinch salt

Also:
Butter, for greasing
Flour, for dusting
4 walnut halves, for garnish
1–2 tsp brown sugar
Icing (confectioners') sugar, for dusting

1 Preheat the oven to 180°C (350°F). Butter a 20 cm (8 inch) springform tin and dust with flour. Invert the tin and tap lightly to get rid of excess flour.

2 Finely chop the walnuts. Whisk the egg yolks, butter and sugar until foamy. Stir in the ground hazelnuts, quark, vanilla seeds, apple juice and cinnamon. Add the salt to the egg whites and beat until stiff. Gently fold the egg whites into the batter, along with the walnuts.

3 Spoon the batter into the tin, smooth the top and bake for about 40 minutes. Remove the tin from the oven. Top the cake with the walnut halves, sprinkle with brown sugar and bake for another 15–20 minutes. Use a toothpick to test for doneness (see page 10). If the cake gets dark too quickly, move the tin to the bottom rack and loosely cover the cake with foil.

4 Leave the cake to cool briefly. Remove from the tin and set aside to cool completely. Dust with icing sugar to serve.

RICOTTA AND BLACKBERRY STRUDEL

MAKES ONE 25 CM (10 INCH) STRUDEL

2 cups (250 g) blackberries
2 eggs, separated
1 pinch salt
1½ cups (350 g) ricotta
150 g (5½ oz) butter, melted
¼ cup (50 g) sugar
1½ tbsp vanilla sugar
Grated zest of 1 lime
1½ tbsp cornflour
¼ cup (35 g) breadcrumbs
2 tbsp brown sugar
7 sheets filo pastry, about 30 x 31 cm (12 x 12½ inches)

Also:
1 egg
2 tbsp milk
Vanilla ice cream, to serve

1 Preheat the oven to 190°C (375°F) and line a large baking tray with baking paper. Gently pick through and wash the blackberries and pat dry.

2 Whisk the egg whites and salt until stiff. Whisk the ricotta with one-third of the melted butter, the egg yolks, sugar, vanilla sugar, lime zest and cornflour. Carefully fold in the beaten egg whites.

3 Combine the breadcrumbs and brown sugar. Spread some paper towel on your work surface. Place one sheet of filo pastry on the paper towel. Brush with melted butter and sprinkle with a little of the breadcrumb mixture. Top with another pastry sheet, brush again with melted butter and sprinkle with the breadcrumb mixture. Repeat with all of the remaining pastry sheets.

4 Spread the ricotta mixture over the top pastry sheet, leaving a 4 cm (1½ inch) edge all around. Spread the blackberries evenly over the filling. Fold the short pastry edges over the filling, then use the paper towel to help roll up the strudel from the bottom, away from you. Transfer the strudel to the baking tray, seam side down.

5 Whisk the egg and milk and brush over the strudel. Bake until golden brown, about 25 minutes. Leave to cool for at least 30 minutes before serving. Serve with vanilla ice cream.

PINEAPPLE MUFFINS WITH COCONUT CRUMBLE

MAKES 12

2 tbsp butter, softened
100 g (3½ oz) sugar
1½ tbsp vanilla sugar
2 eggs
1¼ cups (185 g) plain flour
⅓ cup (40 g) blanched, ground almonds
1 tsp baking powder
1 pinch salt
Grated zest of 1 lime
½ cup (125 ml) coconut milk
150 g (5½ oz) pineapple, finely diced

For the crumble:
½ cup (75 g) plain flour
2 tbsp brown sugar
2½ tbsp butter, softened
⅓ cup (30 g) desiccated coconut

Also:
Desiccated coconut, for sprinkling

1 Preheat the oven to 180°C (350°F). Line a 12-hole muffin tin with paper cases.

2 Whisk the butter with the sugar and vanilla sugar, then whisk in the eggs. Combine the flour, ground almonds, baking powder, salt and lime zest. Stir the dry ingredients into the egg mixture in batches, alternating with the coconut milk. Fold in the diced pineapple. Distribute the batter among the muffin holes, filling them a little over halfway.

3 Quickly rub the crumble ingredients together to make chunky crumbs. Sprinkle the crumble on top of the batter in the muffin holes.

4 Bake the muffins until golden brown, about 20–22 minutes. Remove from the oven and leave to cool completely. Peel off the paper cases and serve sprinkled with desiccated coconut.

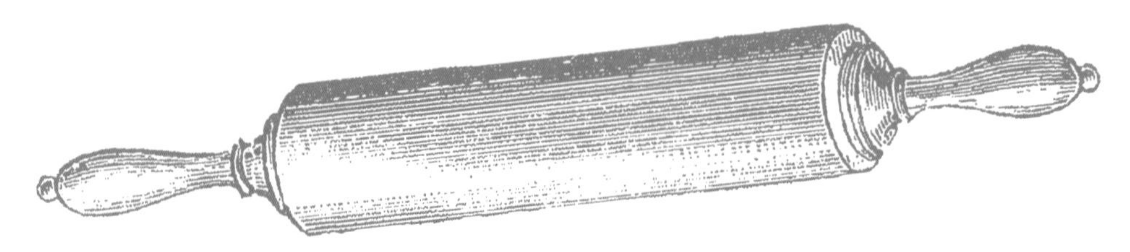

CRANBERRY AND ALMOND TRAY CAKE

1 Preheat the oven to 180°C (350°F). Line a 20 x 30 cm (8 x 12 inch) cake tin with baking paper.

2 For the base, whisk the butter and sugar until creamy. Combine the flour, ground almonds, cornflour and salt in a separate bowl and add to the butter mixture. Combine everything to a soft dough. Transfer the dough to a lightly floured surface and roll out to the size of the tin or gently press flat with your hands. Line the tin with the dough. Prick the base all over with a fork and bake for about 17 minutes. Leave to cool.

3 Spread the cooled base with the cranberries, leaving a small border all around. Whisk the butter and sugar until creamy, then stir in the orange zest and eggs. Combine the ground almonds, flour, baking powder and salt in a separate bowl and quickly stir into the wet mixture.

4 Spoon the mixture on top of the cranberries and level. Sprinkle with half the brown sugar and bake for 10 minutes. Remove from the oven, sprinkle with the flaked almonds and bake for another 25–30 minutes. Use a toothpick to test for doneness (see page 10). If the almond flakes get too dark, loosely cover the tin with foil towards the end of the baking time.

5 Remove the cake from the oven and immediately sprinkle with the remaining brown sugar. Leave to cool in the tin before cutting into individual pieces.

MAKES ONE 20 X 30 CM (8 X 12 INCH) CAKE

For the base:
220 g (7¾ oz) butter, softened
⅓ cup (70 g) sugar
1⅓ cups (200 g) plain flour
¼ cup (30 g) ground almonds
50 g (1¾ oz) cornflour
1 pinch salt

For the topping:
400 g (14 oz) frozen cranberries, thawed and drained
½ cup (120 g) butter, softened
120 g (4¼ oz) sugar
Grated zest of 1 orange
2 eggs
1⅔ cups (170 g) ground almonds
¼ cup (30 g) plain flour
¼ tsp baking powder
1 pinch salt
¼ cup (45 g) brown sugar
About ⅓ cup (30 g) flaked almonds

Also:
Flour, for dusting

CHOCOLATE AND ESPRESSO BISCOTTI

MAKES ABOUT 16

100 g (3½ oz) dark chocolate
50 g (1¾ oz) butter
1 egg
⅓ cup (80 g) sugar
1½ tbsp vanilla sugar
25 ml (¾ fl oz) freshly brewed espresso, cooled
⅔ cup (100 g) plain flour
1½ tbsp cocoa powder
½ tsp baking powder
1 pinch salt

Also:
About ¼ cup (30 g) icing (confectioners') sugar, for rolling

1 Coarsely chop half of the chocolate and finely chop the other half. Melt the coarsely chopped chocolate with the butter in a saucepan over low heat. Whisk the egg, sugar and vanilla sugar until light and creamy. Stir in the chocolate and butter mixture and the espresso.

2 Combine the flour, cocoa powder, baking powder and salt and quickly stir into the wet mixture. Fold in the finely chopped chocolate. Cover the dough and refrigerate for at least 2 hours until it is firm enough to shape into balls.

3 Preheat the oven to 180°C (350°F) and line a baking tray with baking paper. Sift the icing sugar into a deep plate. Shape the dough into 4 cm (1½ inch) balls and roll them in the icing sugar. Transfer the balls onto the baking tray, allowing plenty of room for spreading. Bake the biscotti for 14–18 minutes. They may still seem a little soft, but will firm up as they cool.

NECTARINE AND MARZIPAN TARTLETS

MAKES ABOUT 8

2 sheets puff pastry, thawed
1 egg, lightly beaten
140 g (5 oz) marzipan paste
4–6 ripe nectarines
1 sprig rosemary
⅓ cup (60 g) brown sugar
1½ tbsp vanilla sugar
½ tsp ground cinnamon
¼ tsp ground cardamom
½ tsp grated orange zest

Also:
¼ cup (30 g) chopped hazelnuts
1½ tbsp cold butter
Honey, for drizzling
Icing (confectioners') sugar, for dusting

1 Preheat the oven to 200°C (400°F) and line a baking tray with baking paper. Lay the pastry sheets on a work surface and roll them out a little thinner. Use a large cookie cutter to cut out eight 10 cm (4 inch) discs. Transfer the pastry discs onto the baking tray. Prick the centre of each disc with a fork, leaving a 2 cm (¾ inch) border. Brush the edges with the beaten egg.

2 Finely grate the marzipan and divide among the pastry discs, leaving the edges clear. Wash, dry and halve the nectarines. Remove the stones and slice thinly. Rinse the rosemary and shake off the excess water. Pick off and finely chop the leaves. Combine the rosemary, brown sugar, vanilla sugar, cinnamon, cardamom and orange zest and toss the sliced nectarines in the mixture. Arrange the nectarines on top of the marzipan, with the slices overlapping.

3 Scatter the chopped hazelnuts over the nectarines. Dot the butter on top of the fruit. Drizzle each tartlet with a little honey and bake until golden brown, about 15–20 minutes. Remove from the oven and leave to cool until just warm. Dust with icing sugar and serve.

Mother Holle

ICING SUGAR AND CHOCOLATE

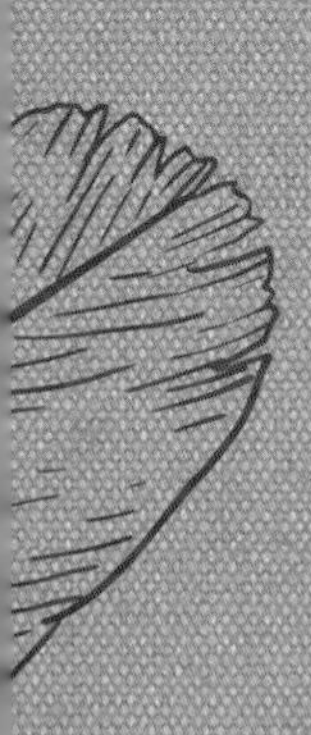

Once upon a time there was a widow, who had two daughters.

One of them was beautiful and industrious, the other ugly and lazy. The mother, however, loved the ugly and lazy one best, because she was her own daughter, and so the other, who was only her stepdaughter, was made to do all the work of the house, and was quite the Cinderella of the family. Her stepmother sent her out every day to sit by the well in the high road, there to spin until she made her fingers bleed. Now it chanced one day that some blood fell on to the spindle, and as the girl stopped over the well to wash it off, the spindle suddenly sprang out of her hand and fell into the well. She ran home crying to tell of her misfortune, but her stepmother spoke harshly to her, and after giving her a violent scolding, said unkindly, 'As you have let the spindle fall into the well, you may go yourself and fetch it out.'

The girl went back to the well not knowing what to do, and at last in her distress she jumped into the water after the spindle.

She remembered nothing more until she awoke and found herself in a beautiful meadow, full of sunshine, and with countless flowers blooming in every direction.

She walked over the meadow, and presently she came upon a baker's oven full of bread, and the loaves cried out to her, 'Take us out, take us out, or alas! we shall be burnt to a cinder; we were baked through long ago.' So she took the bread-shovel and drew them all out.

She went on a little farther, till she came to a tree full of apples. 'Shake me, shake me, I pray,' cried the tree; 'my apples, one and all, are ripe.' So she shook the tree, and the apples came falling down upon her like rain; but she continued shaking until there was not a single apple left upon it. Then she carefully gathered all the apples together into a heap and walked on again.

The next thing she came to was a little house, and there she saw an old woman looking out, with such large teeth that she was terrified, and turned to run away. But the old woman called after her, 'What are you afraid of, dear child? Stay with me; if you will do the work of my house properly for me, I will make you very happy. You must be very careful, however, to make my bed in the right way, for I wish you always to shake it thoroughly, so that the feathers fly about; then they say, down there in the world, that it is snowing; for I am Mother Holle.' The old woman spoke so kindly, that the girl summoned up courage and agreed to enter into her service.

She took care to do everything according to the old woman's bidding and every time she made the bed she shook it with all her might, so that the feathers flew about like so many snowflakes. The old woman was as good as her word: she never spoke angrily to her, and gave her roast and boiled meats every day.

So she stayed on with Mother Holle for some time, and then she began to grow unhappy. She could not at first tell why she felt sad, but she became conscious at last of a great longing to go home; then she knew she was homesick, although she was a thousand times better off with Mother Holle than with her mother and sister. After waiting awhile, she went to Mother Holle and said, 'I am so homesick, that I cannot stay with you any longer, for although I am so happy here, I must return to my own people.'

Then Mother Holle said, 'I am pleased that you should want to go back to your own people, and as you have served me so well and faithfully, I will take you home myself.'

'COCK-A-DOODLE-DOO! YOUR GOLDEN DAUGHTER'S COME BACK TO YOU.'

Thereupon she led the girl by the hand up to a broad gateway. The gate was opened, and as the girl passed through, a shower of gold fell upon her, and the gold clung to her, so that she was covered with it from head to foot.

'That is a reward for your industry,' said Mother Holle, and as she spoke she handed her the spindle that she had dropped into the well.

The gate was then closed, and the girl found herself back in the old world close to her mother's house. As she entered the courtyard, the cock, who was perched on the well, called out:

'Cock-a-doodle-doo!
Your golden daughter's come back to you.'

Then she went in to her mother and sister, and as she was so richly covered with gold, they gave her a warm welcome. She related to them all that had happened, and when the mother heard how she had come by her great riches, she thought she should like her ugly, lazy daughter to go and try her fortune. So she made the sister go and sit by the well and spin, and the

'DO YOU THINK I AM GOING TO DIRTY MY HANDS FOR YOU?'

girl pricked her finger and thrust her hand into a thorn-bush, so that she might drop some blood on to the spindle; then she threw it into the well, and jumped in herself.

Like her sister she awoke in the beautiful meadow, and walked over it till she came to the oven. 'Take us out, take us out, or alas! we shall be burnt to a cinder; we were baked through long ago,' cried the loaves as before. But the lazy girl answered, 'Do you think I am going to dirty my hands for you?' and walked on.

Presently she came to the apple-tree. 'Shake me, shake me, I pray; my apples, one and all, are ripe,' it cried. But she only answered, 'A nice thing to ask me to do, one of the apples might fall on my head,' and passed on.

At last she came to Mother Holle's house, and as she had heard all about the large teeth from her sister, she was not afraid of them, and engaged herself without delay to the old woman.

The first day she was very obedient and industrious, and exerted herself to please Mother Holle, for she thought of the gold she should get in return. The next day, however, she began to dawdle over her work, and the third day she was more idle still; then she began to lie in bed in the mornings and refused to get up. Worse still, she neglected to make the old woman's bed properly, and forgot to shake it so that the feathers might fly about. So Mother Holle very soon got tired of her, and told her she might go. The lazy girl was delighted at this, and thought to herself, 'The gold will soon be mine.' Mother Holle led her, as she had led her sister, to the broad gateway; but as she was passing through, instead of the shower of gold, a great bucketful of pitch came pouring over her.

'That is in return for your services,' said the old woman, and she shut the gate.

So the lazy girl had to go home covered with pitch, and the cock on the well called out as she saw her:

'Cock-a-doodle-doo!
Your dirty daughter's come back to you.'

But, try what she would, she could not get the pitch off and it stuck to her as long as she lived.

SALTED PEANUT CUPCAKES

MAKES 12

185 g (6½ oz) sugar
¼ cup (55 g) vanilla sugar
3 large eggs
2½ tbsp butter
2½ tbsp milk
2 tbsp crème fraîche
2 tbsp freshly brewed espresso, cooled
50 g (1¾ oz) dark chocolate, melted and cooled
50 g (1¾ oz) smooth peanut butter
1 cup (150 g) plain flour
½ cup (50 g) ground hazelnuts
1½ tsp baking powder
¼ cup (30 g) cocoa powder
1 generous pinch of salt

For the topping:
¼ cup (35 g) custard powder
400 ml (14 fl oz) milk
⅓ cup (70 g) sugar
½ tsp ground cinnamon
1 cup (250 g) smooth peanut butter

Also:
⅓ cup (50 g) roasted, salted peanuts, for garnish
Sea salt flakes, for sprinkling

1 Preheat the oven to 180°C (350°F). Line a 12-hole muffin tin with paper cases.

2 Whisk the sugar, vanilla sugar and eggs until thick and creamy. Melt the butter and combine with the milk, crème fraîche and espresso. Stir into the sugar and egg mixture. Stir in the chocolate and peanut butter. Combine the flour, ground hazelnuts, baking powder, cocoa powder and salt and quickly stir into the batter.

3 Fill the muffin holes two-thirds full with batter. Bake the muffins for 18–20 minutes. Use a toothpick to test for doneness (see page 10), then set aside to cool completely.

4 For the topping, whisk the custard powder, 2½ tablespoons of the milk and 2½ tablespoons of the sugar until smooth. Bring the remaining milk, sugar and cinnamon to the boil and add the custard powder mixture, stirring continuously. Simmer for about 1 minute. Pour the custard into a bowl, cover with plastic wrap and set aside to cool completely. Refrigerate for at least 2 hours.

5 Beat the peanut butter until creamy. Briefly whisk the cooled custard and combine with the peanut butter in batches. Transfer the mixture to a piping bag and pipe the cream on top of the cooled cupcakes. Coarsely chop the peanuts and sprinkle on top, together with the sea salt.

WHITE CHOCOLATE CARAMEL CAKE

MAKES ONE 24 CM (9½ INCH) CAKE

150 g (5½ oz) white chocolate
100 g (3½ oz) butter, plus 1 tbsp extra
⅔ cup (100 g) plain flour
½ cup (50 g) blanched, ground almonds
½ cup (80 g) salted macadamia nuts
175 g (6 oz) sugar
1½ tbsp vanilla sugar
1 pinch salt
4 eggs
100 ml (3½ fl oz) single (pure) cream

Also:
30 g (1 oz) white cooking chocolate, melted, or
white chocolate flakes, for decoration

1 Preheat the oven to 180°C (350°F). Line a 24 cm (9½ inch) square cake tin with baking paper.

2 Break the chocolate into pieces and melt in a bowl over a saucepan of simmering water together with the 100 g butter. Set aside to cool.

3 Combine the flour with the ground almonds. Coarsely chop the macadamia nuts.

4 Combine 75 g (2½ oz) of the sugar with the vanilla sugar and salt. Add to the eggs and whisk until thick and foamy. Gradually stir in first the chocolate mixture and then the flour mixture. Transfer the batter to the tin and sprinkle with the chopped macadamia nuts. Bake for about 17–20 minutes.

5 Meanwhile, bring the cream, remaining 1 tablespoon of butter and remaining sugar to the boil in a small saucepan. Reduce the heat and simmer the mixture to thicken for about 15 minutes, stirring occasionally at first and then continuously, as the caramel sauce can burn very quickly.

6 Remove the cake from the oven and quickly spread the hot, thick caramel sauce evenly on top using a spoon. Return the cake to the oven and bake for another 5 minutes, until golden brown. If you like, switch on the grill function for the last minute to create an even crunchier, darker caramel topping. Leave the cake to cool, then decorate with the melted white chocolate or chocolate flakes and slice into rectangles.

CHOCOLATE PANCAKE STACK

MAKES ONE 16 CM (6¼ INCH) CAKE

1⅓ cups (200 g) plain flour
¼ cup (60 g) caster sugar
¼ cup (30 g) cocoa powder
3 tsp baking powder
2 tbsp butter
3 eggs, separated
1½ cups (375 ml) buttermilk
1 pinch salt

For the filling:
½ cup (125 ml) single (pure) cream
1 cup (250 g) mascarpone
125 g (4½ oz) low-fat quark or Greek-style yogurt
¼ cup (50 g) sugar
¼ cup (55 g) vanilla sugar

Also:
Butter, for frying
100 g (3½ oz) dark chocolate flakes or curls
2 tbsp pistachios, chopped

1 Combine the flour, sugar, cocoa powder and baking powder. Melt the butter in a small saucepan and leave to cool a little. Add the egg yolks, buttermilk and butter to the dry ingredients and combine to make a smooth batter. Whisk the egg whites and salt until stiff. Fold gently into the mixture. Set the batter aside to rest for about 20 minutes.

2 For the filling, whip the cream until stiff. Combine the mascarpone, quark, sugar and vanilla sugar in a separate mixing bowl. Gently fold in the whipped cream. Cover the cream mixture and chill.

3 Melt a little butter in a frying pan over medium heat. Place a 16 cm (6¼ inch) metal cake ring inside the pan. (Alternatively, use the ring from a mini springform tin.) Pour 2 ladlefuls of batter inside the ring. Cook the pancake for 2–3 minutes, until small bubbles start to appear on top. Remove the ring by carefully sliding a sharp knife around the inside. Flip the pancake over and cook until done, about 1–2 minutes. Repeat with the remaining batter, occasionally wiping the pan clean. Leave the pancakes to cool completely.

4 Place one pancake on a small serving plate and spread about 2 tablespoons of the cream mixture on top. Top with another pancake and again spread with the cream mixture. Continue until you have used up all the pancakes and filling. Gently reheat the remaining melted chocolate to a spreadable consistency, if necessary, and brush over the top pancake. Serve the pancake stack garnished with chopped chocolate and pistachios to taste.

CHOCOLATE ROLLS WITH APRICOT SAUCE

MAKES 20

About 1 tbsp cornflour
250 g (9 oz) filo pastry, about 30 x 31 cm (12 x 12½ inches)
Vegetable oil, for deep-frying (see page 9)

For the filling:
¼ cup (50 g) sugar
⅓ cup (75 ml) milk
½ cup (125 ml) single (pure) cream
2 tbsp honey
½ tsp vanilla extract
150 g (5½ oz) dark chocolate
100 g (3½ oz) milk chocolate

For the apricot sauce:
300 g (10½ oz) apricots
2 tbsp orange juice
Honey, to taste
½ tsp vanilla extract

Also:
Icing (confectioners') sugar, for dusting

1 Prepare the filling one day ahead. Heat the sugar with 2 tablespoons water in a small saucepan. Stir until the sugar has dissolved and then continue to cook until caramelised. Once the sugar has taken on a golden brown color, add the milk and cream. Be careful, as the mixture may foam up. Add the honey and vanilla extract and simmer until the caramel has dissolved and the mixture is smooth. Remove the saucepan from the heat. Break both types of chocolate into pieces. Add to the hot caramel and stir to melt. Leave the chocolate filling to cool and then refrigerate for at least 8 hours until it has firmed up.

2 Wash and halve the apricots for the sauce and remove the stones. Use a stick blender to purée the apricots with the orange juice and pass through a fine sieve. Sweeten with honey and flavor with vanilla, to taste.

3 Whisk the cornflour with ⅓ cup (80 ml) cold water to dissolve. Spread a sheet of pastry on your work surface. Brush with a little of the cornflour mixture and place another sheet of pastry on top. Press together well, then cut into quarters. Repeat with the remaining sheets to make a total of 20 pieces, about 15 x 15 cm (6 x 6 inches) each. Brush the edges of the squares with the cornflour mixture. Place 1 tablespoon of the chocolate filling on the bottom third of each square. Fold the sides in towards the centre to cover all of the filling and roll up tightly, starting from the side closest to you. The rolls should measure about 2 x 7.5 cm (¾ x 3 inches). Brush the top edges with the cornflour mixture to seal well and prevent any filling from leaking out during deep-frying.

4 Heat the oil to about 170°C (338°F) in a saucepan or deep-fryer. Deep-fry the rolls in batches, cooking three at a time. Cook for a few minutes until golden brown, moving the rolls around a little with a slotted spoon. Drain on paper towel. Dust with icing sugar and serve warm with the apricot sauce.

MINI LAVA CAKES

MAKES 6–8

½ cup (120 g) butter
100 g (3½ oz) dark chocolate
100 g (3½ oz) milk chocolate
2 eggs
2 egg yolks
2 tbsp sugar
1½ tbsp vanilla sugar
1 tbsp plain flour
2 tbsp cocoa powder
1 pinch salt
About 50 g (1¾ oz) white chocolate

Also:
Butter, for greasing
Cocoa powder, for dusting

1 Preheat the oven to 210°C (410°F). Butter six to eight small silicone baking moulds or ovenproof cups, about 8 cm (3¼ inches in diameter). Dust the moulds with cocoa powder.

2 Melt the butter in a small saucepan. Meanwhile, break both types of chocolate into pieces. Take the saucepan off the heat. Add the chocolate to the melted, hot butter and stir to melt. Leave the mixture to cool.

3 Whisk the eggs, egg yolks, sugar and vanilla sugar for a few minutes until thick and foamy. Slowly stir in the cooled chocolate butter. Combine the flour, cocoa powder and salt and gently fold into the mixture. Divide the batter among the moulds to fill them about three-quarters full. Coarsely chop the white chocolate. Push a few pieces into the centre of each cake, ensuring that the white chocolate is completely covered with batter.

4 Bake the cakes for 8–10 minutes, depending on the mould size. They should still be liquid in the centre. (If you want to be sure, bake a trial lava cake to check how long they take to cook to perfection.)

5 Remove the lava cakes from the oven and leave to cool briefly. Invert onto serving plates and serve warm.

EKCO CHICAGO
PAT. PEND
EKCO CHICAGO
PAT. PEND

HAZELNUT, BEETROOT AND CHOCOLATE MUFFINS

MAKES 12

120 g (4¼ oz) plain flour
½ cup (50 g) ground hazelnuts
150 g (5½ oz) sugar
1½ tbsp vanilla sugar
½ cup (50 g) cocoa powder
2 tsp baking powder
1 pinch salt
200 g (7 oz) cooked beetroot
150 ml (5 fl oz) canola oil
3 eggs

Also:
100 g (3½ oz) dark cooking chocolate
50 g (1¾ oz) icing (confectioners') sugar
About 1½ tbsp beetroot juice
Red food coloring
½ cup (80 g) hazelnuts

1 Preheat the oven to 180°C (350°F). Line two 6-hole or one 12-hole muffin tin with paper cases; alternatively, butter the holes and dust them with flour to get beautifully smooth muffins.

2 Combine the flour, ground hazelnuts, sugar, vanilla sugar, cocoa powder, baking powder and salt. Coarsely chop the beetroot and transfer to a tall mixing bowl together with the oil. Finely blend with a stick blender, then add the eggs one by one. Quickly stir in the dry ingredients in three batches to combine everything well.

3 Divide the batter among the muffin holes, filling them two-thirds full. Bake for about 22 minutes. Use a toothpick to test for doneness (see page 10). Set the muffins aside to cool, then remove from the tins.

4 Melt the dark cooking chocolate in a bowl over a saucepan of simmering water. Whisk the icing sugar, beetroot juice and a little food coloring together to make a bright pink icing. Coarsely chop the hazelnuts and dry-roast in a frying pan until they smell fragrant. Glaze half of the cooled muffins with the chocolate and the other half with the icing. Sprinkle with the nuts.

MINI CHOCOLATE CROISSANTS

MAKES 12

100 g (3½ oz) dark or milk chocolate
80 g (2¾ oz) low-fat quark or Greek-style yogurt
40 g (1½ oz) crème fraîche
¼ cup (50 g) sugar
1½ tbsp vanilla sugar
⅓ cup (75 ml) milk
2½ tbsp canola or sunflower oil
1⅓ cups (200 g) plain flour, plus extra for kneading
60 g (2¼ oz) blanched, ground almonds
1½ tsp baking powder
1 pinch salt

Also:
Flour, for rolling
1 egg yolk, lightly beaten with a little milk
60 g (2¼ oz) dark or milk chocolate

1 Chop the chocolate. Whisk the quark with the crème fraîche, sugar, vanilla sugar, milk and oil. Combine the flour, ground almonds, baking powder and salt and add to the wet ingredients. Knead everything until well combined. Add a little more flour if the dough seems too sticky.

2 Preheat the oven to 180°C (350°F) and line a baking tray with baking paper. Roll out the dough on a lightly floured work surface until about 3 mm (⅛ inch) thick. Cut out triangles about 12 x 14 x 14 cm (4½ x 5½ inches x 5½ inches) in size. Sprinkle the short side with the chopped chocolate, roll up the triangles and shape them into croissants. Transfer the croissants onto the baking tray and brush with the beaten egg. Bake until golden brown, about 20 minutes.

3 Meanwhile, coarsely chop the chocolate and melt it in a bowl set over a saucepan of simmering water. Once the croissants have cooled, dip the ends into the melted chocolate. Set aside to dry.

CHOCOLATE HAZELNUT SWISS ROLL

1 Preheat the oven to 200°C (400°F) and line a baking tray with baking paper. Beat the egg whites, salt and 2 tablepoons cold water until stiff, gradually adding half the caster sugar. Whisk the egg yolks, remaining caster sugar and vanilla sugar until creamy. Gently fold in the beaten egg whites. Sift the flour, cornflour and baking powder on top and fold in gently. Spread the batter over the baking tray, making a rectangle about 30 x 40 cm (12 x 16 inches) and about 7 mm (¼ inch) thick. Bake until golden brown, about 12 minutes.

2 Invert the cooked sponge onto a clean tea towel sprinkled with sugar. Carefully peel off the baking paper. Cover the sponge with a damp tea towel to prevent it from becoming dry and brittle as it cools.

3 For the filling, melt the chocolate hazelnut spread in a bowl set over a saucepan of simmering water. Beat the egg whites until semi-stiff. Gradually add 2 tablespoons of the sugar and continue to beat until stiff. Add the egg yolks, remaining sugar, cocoa powder and milk to a metal bowl and whisk over the pan of simmering water until foamy, about 5 minutes. Do not allow the mixture to get too hot! Meanwhile, soak the gelatine in cold water. Squeeze out excess water and whisk the gelatine into the warm egg yolk mixture to dissolve. Immediately stir in the melted chocolate hazelnut spread, followed by the cream cheese. Carefully fold in the beaten egg whites. Refrigerate the filling for about 30 minutes until it has firmed up a little.

4 Spread the filling over the sponge cake and sprinkle with the chopped hazelnuts. Roll up evenly using the tea towel, starting from a short side. Wrap tightly in foil and refrigerate for at least 1½ hours.

5 For the icing, chop the cooking chocolate. Bring the cream to the boil in a small saucepan. Remove from the heat and add the chocolate, chocolate hazelnut spread and coconut oil and stir to melt. Bring the sugar and 2½ tablespoons water to the boil in a second saucepan. Stir to dissolve, then stir in the chocolate mixture. Leave to cool, then glaze the Swiss roll. Refrigerate for another 1½ hours before serving.

MAKES ONE 30 CM (12 INCH) ROLL

4 eggs, separated
1 pinch salt
¼ cup (50 g) caster sugar
1½ tbsp vanilla sugar
⅓ cup (50 g) plain flour
50 g (1¾ oz) cornflour
¼ tsp baking powder

For the filling:
⅓ cup (100 g) chocolate hazelnut spread
2 eggs, separated
85 g (3 oz) sugar
1½ tbsp cocoa powder
2 tbsp milk
2 gelatine sheets
250 g (9 oz) cream cheese

For the icing:
100 g (3½ oz) dark cooking chocolate
100 ml (3½ fl oz) single (pure) cream
⅓ cup (100 g) chocolate hazelnut spread
25 g (1 oz) coconut oil
¼ cup (50 g) sugar

Also:
Sugar, for rolling
About ⅓ cup (50 g) chopped hazelnuts, for garnish

STRAWBERRY CHOCOLATE TARTLETS WITH PINE NUTS

MAKES 6

For the dough:
125 g (4½ oz) plain flour
⅓ cup (40 g) ground hazelnuts
¼ cup (60 g) mascarpone
¼ cup (60 g) butter, softened
¼ cup (60 g) sugar
2 tbsp cocoa powder
1 pinch salt

For the filling:
50 g (1¾ oz) dark chocolate
50 g (1¾ oz) milk chocolate
2 eggs, separate
⅓ cup (80 g) sugar
¼ cup (55 g) vanilla sugar
2 gelatine sheets
200 g (7 oz) mascarpone
About 1⅔ cups (250 g) strawberries
About 2 tbsp pine nuts

Also:
Butter, for greasing
Cocoa powder, for dusting
Flour, for dusting
Brown sugar and grated chocolate, for sprinkling

1 For the dough, add all ingredients to a mixing bowl and knead well to combine. Shape the dough into a ball, cover with plastic wrap and chill for at least 45 minutes.

2 Preheat the oven to 190°C (375°F). Butter six 10 cm (4 inch) shallow tartlet tins and dust with cocoa powder. Invert the tins and tap lightly to get rid of excess cocoa. Roll out the dough on a lightly floured surface until about 3 mm (⅛ inch) thick. Use a large cookie cutter to cut out discs to line the tins. Prick the bases with a fork and bake the tartlet shells for 12–15 minutes. Remove the tins from the oven and set aside to cool before unmoulding the tartlets.

3 For the filling, coarsely chop both types of chocolate and melt them in a bowl set over a saucepan of simmering water. Beat the egg yolks, half the sugar and the vanilla sugar over the saucepan of simmering water until thick and foamy. Meanwhile, soak the gelatine in cold water. Squeeze out excess water and whisk the gelatine into the warm egg mixture to dissolve. Stir in the melted chocolate. Remove the bowl from the heat and immediately whisk in the mascarpone. Beat the egg whites and remaining sugar until stiff. Gently fold the egg whites into the chocolate mixture. Set the mixture aside for 15 minutes until it starts to set. Divide among the tartlet shells and level the tops. Refrigerate for another 20 minutes. (Any leftover cream makes a delicious dessert.)

4 Thinly slice the strawberries. Dry-roast the pine nuts in a frying pan until golden brown. Divide the sliced strawberries among the tartlets and sprinkle with a little brown sugar, grated chocolate and toasted pine nuts. These tartlets are best served immediately.

CHOCOLATE RING

MAKES ONE 26 CM (10½ INCH) RING

3⅓ cups (500 g) plain flour
100 g (3½ oz) sugar
1½ tbsp vanilla sugar
1 generous pinch of salt
20 g (¾ oz) fresh yeast
100 ml (3½ fl oz) lukewarm milk
3 eggs
125 g (4½ oz) butter, softened

For the filling:
100 g (3½ oz) dark chocolate (70% cocoa)
20 g (¾ oz) milk chocolate
80 g (2¾ oz) butter
⅓ cup (40 g) icing (confectioners') sugar

For the glaze:
⅓ cup (80 g) sugar
1–2 tbsp orange juice

Also:
Flour, for dusting
Icing (confectioners') sugar, for dusting

1 Combine the flour, sugar, vanilla sugar and salt in a mixing bowl. Dissolve the yeast in the lukewarm milk. Add the eggs, softened butter and yeast mixture to the dry ingredients and knead everything for about 8 minutes to make a smooth, pliable dough. Cover the bowl with plastic wrap and leave the dough to rise for about 2 hours.

2 For the filling, coarsely chop both types of chocolate and melt them, together with the butter, in a bowl set over a saucepan of simmering water. Set aside to cool, then whisk in the icing sugar until smooth.

3 Divide the dough into two equal portions. Roll out each piece on a lightly floured surface into a rectangle about 28 x 38 cm (11¼ x 15 inches) in size and 3 mm (⅛ inch) thick. Spread the chocolate filling evenly over the dough, leaving a 2 cm (¾ inch) border on all sides. Roll up the dough tightly and evenly, starting from the narrow side. Trim the ends and join both rolls together to make a ring. Press the ends together gently, then use a sharp knife to score the top in a zigzag pattern. Transfer the ring to a baking tray lined with baking paper. Cover the tray with plastic wrap and leave the dough to rise for another 30 minutes.

4 Preheat the oven to 180°C (350°F). Bake the chocolate ring for about 35 minutes. If the surface gets too dark, cover with foil and transfer to the bottom rack of the oven.

5 Meanwhile, for the glaze, bring the sugar to the boil in a small saucepan together with the orange juice and 2 tablespoons water. Simmer over low heat to reduce for about 8 minutes, stirring occasionally. Remove the chocolate ring from the oven and drizzle with the glaze while still hot. Set aside to cool completely before slicing. Serve the ring dusted with icing sugar.

Rausch

CHOCOLATE MOUSSE FLANS

MAKES 7

For the sponge:
3 eggs
2 tbsp sugar
1½ tbsp vanilla sugar
⅓ cup (50 g) plain flour
2 tsp baking powder
¼ cup (25 g) cocoa powder

For the mousse:
100 g (3½ oz) milk chocolate
75 g (2½ oz) dark chocolate (min. 60% cocoa)
350 ml (12 fl oz) single (pure) cream
2 eggs
1½ tbsp sugar
2 gelatine sheets

Also:
About 100 g (3½ oz) dark chocolate, melted (optional)
About 150 ml (5 fl oz) single (pure) cream and 1–2 tsp icing (confectioners') sugar (or use meringue kisses)
Cocoa powder, for dusting

1 For the sponge, preheat the oven to 180°C (350°F) and line a 26 cm (10½ inch) springform tin with baking paper. Whisk the eggs, sugar and vanilla sugar together until foamy, about 5 minutes. Combine the flour, baking powder and cocoa powder and quickly fold into the egg mixture. Transfer the batter to the springform tin and bake for about 15 minutes. Leave to cool. Use a cookie cutter to cut out seven discs from the sponge, about 5 cm (2 inches) in diameter. Place seven 5 cm (2 inch) pastry rings on a tray. Place a sponge disc inside each ring.

2 For the mousse, melt both types of chocolate in a bowl set over a saucepan of simmering water. Whip the cream until stiff. Place the eggs, sugar and ⅓ cup (80 ml) water in a bowl and place over the simmering water. Whisk until thick and creamy, about 5 minutes. Meanwhile, soak the gelatine in cold water. Squeeze out excess water from the gelatine and whisk it into the warm egg mixture, along with the melted chocolate. Remove the bowl from the pan and set aside to cool. Gently fold in the whipped cream and refrigerate the mousse for about 20 minutes. Divide the mousse among the sponge bases and refrigerate the flans for about 2 hours.

3 Carefully slide a very thin, sharp knife around the insides of the rings and gently lift them off the flans. Glaze the sides of the flans with the cooled, melted dark chocolate, if using. Whip the cream and icing sugar until stiff. Transfer to a piping bag and pipe cream kisses on top of the flans. If using meringue kisses, use a kitchen torch to color the kisses to your taste. Dust with cocoa powder to serve.

MARZIPAN CHOCOLATE ROLLS

MAKES 15–20

For the filling:
2 tbsp butter, softened
1 tbsp sugar
1½ tbsp vanilla sugar
1 egg
⅓ cup (50 g) plain flour
2 tsp cocoa powder
¼ tsp baking powder
1 pinch salt
1 tbsp Amaretto

For the rolls:
100 g (3½ oz) dark cooking chocolate
250 g (9 oz) marzipan paste
1 tbsp butter, softened
¼ cup (30 g) icing (confectioners') sugar
1 tbsp Amaretto

Also:
Butter, for greasing

1 For the filling, preheat the oven to 180°C (350°F). Butter an 18 cm (7 inch) springform tin, or two holes of a muffin tin. (If using a muffin tin, you may need to shorten the baking time.) Whisk the butter, sugar and vanilla sugar until creamy. Stir in the egg. Combine the flour, cocoa powder, baking powder and salt in a separate bowl. Stir the dry ingredients and Amaretto into the egg mixture. Transfer the batter to the tin or tray and bake for about 18 minutes. Set aside to cool briefly, then remove from the tin and leave to cool completely. Once cooled, finely crumble in a food processor or between your fingers.

2 For the rolls, coarsely chop the cooking chocolate and melt in a bowl set over a saucepan of simmering water. Finely dice 25 g (1 oz) of the marzipan and combine with the butter and icing sugar. Stir in 40 g (1½ oz) of the melted chocolate, the Amaretto and cake crumbs. Knead everything together with your hands until well combined. Shape into a ball and refrigerate.

3 Divide the remaining marzipan into two even portions. Roll each portion out on baking paper to make a rectangle about 7 x 24 cm (2¾ x 9½ inches) in size, about 3 mm (⅛ inch) thick.

4 Divide the filling into two even portions and shape each portion into a roll about 24 cm (9½ inches) long. Place the rolls on the centre of the marzipan sheets. Use the baking paper to roll the marzipan tightly around the rolls. Press the edges together to seal. Slice into pieces about 2.5 cm (1 inch) long. Dip one end of each piece into the remaining melted chocolate and leave to set.

BLACK AND WHITE CAKE

MAKES ONE 24 CM (9½ INCH) LOAF

6 eggs, separated
1 pinch salt
1 cup (250 g) butter, softened
180 g (6 oz) sugar
¼ cup (55 g) vanilla sugar
280 g (10 oz) plain flour
50 g (1¾ oz) cornflour
2 tbsp cocoa powder
1 tbsp milk

For the icing:
200 g (7 oz) dark cooking chocolate
100 ml (3½ fl oz) single (pure) cream
2 tsp coconut oil
1½ tbsp sugar
50 g (1¾ oz) white cooking chocolate

Also:
Butter, for greasing
Flour, for dusting

1 Preheat the oven to 250°C (500°F). Butter a 24 cm (9½ inch) loaf tin and dust with flour. Invert the tin and tap lightly to get rid of excess flour. Beat the egg whites and salt until stiff. Whisk the egg yolks, butter, sugar and vanilla sugar until foamy. Combine the flour with the cornflour and stir into the egg yolk mixture in three batches. Carefully fold in the beaten egg whites. Divide the batter into two equal portions. (This is best done using your kitchen scales.) Stir the cocoa and milk into one half of the batter.

2 Spread 3–4 tablespoons of the dark batter over the base of the tin. Level the top and bake for 4–5 minutes. Add 3–4 tablespoons of the light batter and bake again. Continue until you have layered and baked all of both batters. (If you want to be very precise, weigh each layer to make sure they all have exactly the same thickness.) Once you have baked the last layer, cover the tin with foil and bake for another 5–10 minutes. Remove from the oven and leave to cool in the tin before inverting the cake carefully onto a wire rack. Set aside to cool completely.

3 For the icing, chop the dark chocolate. Heat the cream in a saucepan, add the chopped chocolate, coconut oil and sugar and stir to melt. Once combined, remove from the heat and set aside to cool for about 10 minutes, stirring occasionally. Glaze the cake all over with the chocolate mixture. Finely chop the white chocolate and place in a small resealable plastic bag. Seal the bag and immerse in hot water until the chocolate has melted. Pat the bag dry, cut off a small corner and pipe the liquid chocolate across the dark chocolate glaze in fine lines. Use a toothpick to marble the glaze. Refrigerate the cake for about 2 hours until the glaze has set.

CHOCOLATE BOURBON CUPCAKES

MAKES 12

100 g (3½ oz) walnuts
120 g (4¼ oz) sugar
2 tbsp hot water
½ cup (125 g) butter, softened
1½ tbsp vanilla sugar
2 eggs
1⅓ cups (180 g) plain flour
⅓ cup (40 g) cocoa powder
¼ tsp salt
2 tsp baking powder
⅓ cup (75 ml) milk
50 ml (1½ fl oz) Bourbon whiskey

For the topping:
2 cups (500 ml) milk
1 cup (250 ml) single (pure) cream
60 g (2¼ oz) custard powder
1 tbsp cocoa powder
1½ tbsp sugar
¾ cup (180 g) butter, softened

For the Bourbon caramel sauce:
⅓ cup (75 g) sugar
2 tbsp single (pure) cream
25 ml (¾ fl oz) Bourbon whiskey

1 For the topping, whisk the milk and cream together with the custard powder, cocoa powder and sugar in a saucepan. Bring the mixture to the boil and simmer, stirring continuously, until it thickens. Transfer the custard to a bowl, cover immediately with plastic wrap and leave to cool completely. Refrigerate for at least 1 hour.

2 Meanwhile, preheat the oven to 180°C (350°F) and line a baking tray with baking paper. Finely grind half of the walnuts in a high-powered blender or grinder. Chop the remaining nuts. Dissolve 2 tablespoons of the sugar in the hot water and toss with the chopped nuts. Transfer the mixture to the baking tray in a single layer and roast for about 10 minutes, turning once. Leave to cool. Don't turn off the oven.

3 Beat the butter until creamy. Whisk in the remaining sugar and vanilla sugar. Whisk the eggs in one by one. Combine the flour, cocoa powder, salt, baking powder and ground walnuts. Combine the milk and Bourbon in a separate bowl. Stir the Bourbon mixture and the dry ingredients into the egg mixture, alternating between the two. Do not overmix. Fold in the caramelised, roasted walnuts.

4 Line a 12-hole muffin tin with paper cases. Divide the batter among the holes, filling them three-quarters full. Bake for 18–20 minutes. Use a toothpick to test for doneness (see page 10). Set aside to cool a little before removing from the tin. Leave the muffins to cool completely.

5 For the topping, whip the butter until light and creamy. Stir the cold, firm custard until smooth. Slowly add the custard to the butter, one tablespoon at a time, to make a pipeable cream. Transfer the cream to a piping bag and pipe on top of the cooled muffins.

6 For the Bourbon caramel sauce, caramelise the sugar in a small saucepan until light brown, stirring continuously. Whisk in the cream and simmer briefly until well combined and glossy. Remove from the heat and stir in the Bourbon. Set aside to cool, then use a teaspoon to drizzle the sauce over the muffins. Serve these cupcakes immediately.

The Star-Money

DIVINE BAKING

There was once upon a time a little girl...

...whose father and mother were dead, and she was so poor that she no longer had any little room to live in, or bed to sleep in, and at last she had nothing else but the clothes she was wearing and a little bit of bread in her hand, which some charitable soul had given her. She was, however, good and pious. And as she was thus forsaken by all the world, she went forth into the open country, trusting in the good God. Then a poor man met her, who said, 'Ah, give me something to eat, I am so hungry!' She handed him the whole of her piece of bread, and said, 'May God bless it to thy use,' and went onwards. Then came a child who moaned and said, 'My head is so cold, give me something to cover it with.' So she took off her hood and gave it to him; and when she had walked a little farther, she met another child who had no jacket and was frozen with cold. Then she gave it her own; and a little farther on one begged for a frock, and she gave away that also. At length she got into a forest and it had already become dark, and there came yet another child, and asked for a little shirt, and the good little girl thought to herself, 'It is a dark night and no one sees thee, thou canst very well give thy little shirt away,' and took it off, and gave away that also. And as she so stood, and had not one single thing left, suddenly some stars from heaven fell down, and they were nothing else but hard smooth pieces of money, and although she had just given her little shirt away, she had a new one that was of the very finest linen. Then she gathered together the money into this, and was rich all the days of her life.

ANGEL EYES

MAKES ABOUT 20

1 cup (150 g) plain flour
⅓ cup (30 g) ground almonds
¼ cup (60 g) sugar
½ tsp baking powder
1 pinch ground cinnamon
½ tsp grated lemon zest
1 pinch salt
75 g (2½ oz) cold butter
1 egg

Also:
About ¼ cup (85 g) strained raspberry jam or raspberry jelly
Icing (confectioners') sugar, for dusting

1 Combine the flour, ground almonds, sugar, baking powder, cinnamon, lemon zest and salt in a mixing bowl. Dice the butter and rub into the flour until the mixture resembles coarse breadcrumbs. Add the egg and knead everything together until well combined. Shape the dough into a ball, cover with plastic wrap and chill for 30 minutes.

2 Divide the dough into walnut-sized pieces and shape into balls. Transfer the balls onto a large tray and use the handle of a wooden spoon to make a well in each. Refrigerate the dough balls for another 30 minutes.

3 Preheat the oven to 180°C (350°F). Line a baking tray with baking paper. Arrange the dough balls on the tray, spacing them a little apart, and fill the wells with raspberry jam. Bake for about 10 minutes. Remove from the oven and leave to cool on a wire rack. (If you like, top up the wells with a little more jam, as the filling sometimes subsides a little.) Serve dusted with icing sugar.

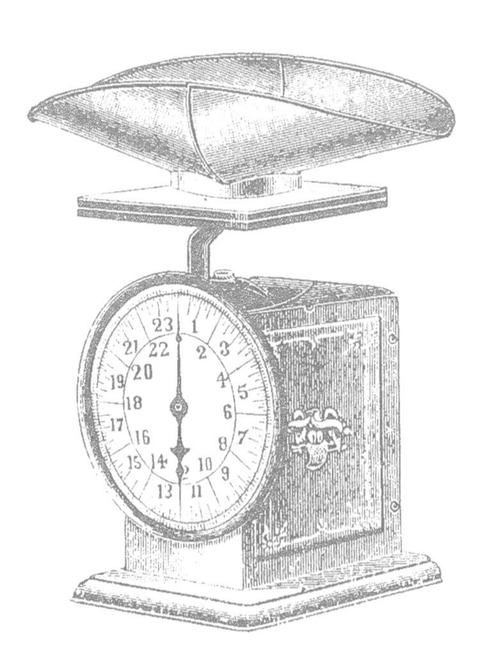

SWEET POTATO AND MASCARPONE PIE

MAKES ONE 24 CM (9½ INCH) PIE

275 g (9¾ oz) plain flour
¼ tsp salt
2½ tsp brown sugar
150 g (5½ oz) cold butter

For the filling:
450 g (1 lb) peeled sweet potatoes
70 ml (2¼ fl oz) orange juice
1–2 tsp butter
½ cup (120 ml) single (pure) cream
2 large eggs
1 large egg yolk
100 g (3½ oz) brown sugar
1 tbsp honey
⅓ cup (85 g) mascarpone
1 tsp ground cinnamon
¼ tsp ground cardamom
¼ tsp freshly grated nutmeg
1 pinch ground allspice

Also:
Butter, for greasing
Flour, for dusting
Dried beans, for blind baking
Ground cinnamon, for dusting

1 Butter a 24 cm (9½ inch) loose-based pie tin and dust with flour. Invert the tin and tap lightly to get rid of excess flour.

2 Combine the flour, salt and brown sugar. Dice the butter and rub into the flour mixture until the mixture resembles coarse breadcrumbs. Add 2–3 tablespoons cold water and knead until well combined. Roll out the dough into a circle on a lightly floured surface. Line the pie tin with the dough. Prick the base all over with a fork and chill for about 30 minutes.

3 Meanwhile, dice the sweet potato for the filling. Transfer to a saucepan together with the orange juice, a little water and the butter. Briefly bring to the boil, then cover and simmer over low heat for about 20 minutes or until soft. Stir occasionally to make sure the filling does not burn. Add a little more water if needed. Transfer the sweet potato to a beaker together with the cream and purée with a stick blender. Leave to cool.

4 Preheat the oven to 200°C (400°F). Line the pie base with baking paper and top with dry beans. Blind bake for 12–14 minutes. Reduce the oven to 180°C (350°F). Remove the baking paper and beans and leave the base to cool.

5 Whisk the eggs, egg yolk and brown sugar in a large bowl until foamy. Stir in the puréed sweet potato and cream mixture, honey, mascarpone, cinnamon, cardamom, nutmeg and allspice until you have a smooth, creamy mixture. Spread the mixture evenly over the pie base to come up almost to the edge. You may have a little filling left over, depending on how deep your tin is. Bake for 35–40 minutes. Cover the pie with foil if the edges turn too dark. Leave to cool completely before removing the pie from the tin. Dust with cinnamon.

PEACH ROSE CUPS

SERVES 8

For the puff pastry roses:
3 peaches
1 tsp butter
¼ cup (85 g) peach jam
2 sheets (270 g/9½ oz) puff pastry
1 tbsp brown sugar

For the cream:
7 peaches
Grated zest and juice of ½ lemon
⅓ cup (80 g) jam-setting sugar (3:1)
2 tsp rose petal syrup
400 g (14 oz) yogurt cream cheese (labneh)
400 g (14 oz) low-fat quark or Greek-style yogurt
2 tbsp icing (confectioners') sugar
¼ cup (55 g) vanilla sugar
1 cup (250 ml) single (pure) cream

Also:
Icing (confectioners') sugar, for dusting

1 For the puff pastry roses, preheat the oven to 190°C (375°F). Line eight holes of a muffin tin with paper cases. Wash, pat dry and halve the peaches. Remove the stones and slice very thinly. If the peaches are very firm, melt the butter in a frying pan and stew the sliced peaches for a few minutes until soft. Gently warm the jam until it softens.

2 Roll out the puff pastry on your work surface and cut it into eight strips about 4.5 cm (1¾ inches) wide. Lightly brush the pastry strips with jam and layer the sliced peaches on top, slightly overlapping, so that the tops of the slices extend above the pastry on the top long side. Sprinkle the peaches with brown sugar. Gently fold the bottom long side over the sliced peaches and roll up tightly from one of the short sides. Transfer the resulting roses to the muffin tin and brush with the remaining jam. Bake for about 50 minutes until the pastry roses have crisped up and taken on a golden brown color. If they turn too dark, cover them with foil for the final 15 minutes of baking time. Set aside to cool before gently unmoulding the roses from the tins.

3 For the cream, peel and halve the peaches and remove the stones. Dice and finely blend together with the lemon juice. You will need about 2 cups (500 ml) peach purée. Stir the jam-setting sugar into the peach purée in a small saucepan and heat. Simmer for a few minutes, stirring continuously. Remove the saucepan from the heat and stir in the rose petal syrup. Set aside to cool completely. Mix the cream cheese, quark, lemon zest, icing sugar and vanilla sugar together with ½ cup (125 ml) of the peach purée until smooth. Whip the cream until stiff and fold into the cream cheese mixture. Layer the cream and peach purée in eight dessert glasses or a large glass bowl. Top with the pastry roses and dust with icing sugar for serving.

REDCURRANT BOMBE

SERVES 6–8

For the sponge:
3 eggs, separated
1 pinch salt
100 g (3½ oz) sugar
60 g (2¼ oz) plain flour
⅓ cup (40 g) cornflour
¼ tsp baking powder
200 g (7 oz) redcurrant jelly

For the filling:
300 g (10½ oz) fresh redcurrants (or thawed and drained frozen redcurrants)
2 tbsp lime juice
Grated zest of ½ lime
400 g (14 oz) cream cheese
300 g (10½ oz) low-fat quark or Greek-style yogurt
125 g (4½ oz) sugar
7 gelatine sheets
100 ml (3½ fl oz) single (pure) cream
1½ tbsp vanilla sugar

For the shortcrust pastry:
¾ cup (110 g) plain flour
2 tbsp sugar
1½ tbsp vanilla sugar
1 pinch salt
75 g (2½ oz) cold butter, diced
1 egg yolk

Also:
Fresh redcurrants, for garnish

1 For the sponge, preheat the oven to 200°C (400°F) and line a baking tray with baking paper. Beat the egg whites and salt until semi-stiff. Gradually add half of the sugar and beat until stiff. Whisk the egg yolks and remaining sugar until light and creamy. Combine the flour, cornflour and baking powder and fold into the beaten egg whites in batches, alternating with the egg yolk mixture. Spread the batter over the baking tray about 6 mm (¼ inch) thick and bake for about 9 minutes. Invert onto a damp tea towel and remove the baking paper. Cover the sponge with another damp tea towel and set aside to cool.

2 For the filling, wash the redcurrants and pick them off the stems. Set aside one-third of the redcurrants. Blend the remainder with the lime juice and strain the purée through a fine sieve. Combine the lime zest, cream cheese, quark and sugar. Soak the gelatine in cold water. Squeeze out excess water and dissolve the gelatine in a saucepan over low heat. Stir 2 tablespoons of the cream cheese mixture into the gelatine, then add the gelatine mixture to the remaining cream to combine. Fold in the redcurrant purée and whole berries. Refrigerate the cream mixture for 20 minutes. Whip the cream until stiff, gradually adding the vanilla sugar, then quickly fold into the redcurrant cream.

3 Warm the redcurrant jelly and spread it over the sponge. Halve the sponge lengthwise and roll up each half tightly and evenly, starting from the narrow side. Wrap the rolls in foil and refrigerate for 20 minutes. Line a bowl with plastic wrap. Slice the sponge rolls and line the bowl tightly with the slices. Trim the slices to give an even edge. Add the redcurrant filling to the bowl. Cover and refrigerate for at least 3 hours.

4 For the pastry, combine the flour, sugar, vanilla sugar and salt in a mixing bowl. Add the butter and rub in until the mixture resembles coarse breadcrumbs. Add the egg yolk and knead until well combined. Wrap the dough in plastic wrap and refrigerate for 30 minutes. Preheat the oven to 200°C (400°F) and line a 24 cm (9½ inch) springform tin with baking paper. Roll the dough out into a circle on the plastic wrap. Transfer to the springform tin and bake for 10 minutes. Leave to cool.

5 Place the base on top of the filling and carefully invert the bombe onto a serving plate. Garnish with fresh redcurrants.

MACADAMIA CUPCAKES

MAKES 12

145 g (5 oz) butter, softened
75 g (2½ oz) brown sugar
1½ tbsp vanilla sugar
3 large eggs
70 ml (2¼ fl oz) maple syrup
210 g (7½ oz) plain flour
2 tsp baking powder
⅓ cup (80 ml) milk
85 g (3 oz) salted macadamia nuts

For the topping:
150 g (5½ oz) butter, softened
2 tsp maple syrup
¼ tsp ground cinnamon
2 cups (250 g) icing (confectioners') sugar
75 g (2½ oz) cream cheese
1½ tbsp roughly chopped salted macadamia nuts
1 tsp raw sugar

Also:
Maple syrup, for drizzling

1 Preheat the oven to 180°C (350°F). Line a 12-hole muffin tin with paper cases.

2 Whisk the butter, brown sugar and vanilla sugar until creamy, then add the eggs one by one. Stir in the maple syrup. Combine the flour and baking powder and stir in quickly, along with the milk. Chop the macadamia nuts and fold in.

3 Divide the batter among the muffin holes. Bake for 18–20 minutes. Use a toothpick to test for doneness (see page 10). Set the cupcakes aside to cool briefly, then remove from the tin and leave to cool completely.

4 For the topping, whip the butter until light and creamy. Stir in 1 teaspoon of the maple syrup and the cinnamon. Gradually incorporate the icing sugar, followed by the cream cheese. Refrigerate the mixture for about 20 minutes. Transfer to a piping bag and pipe on top of the cooled cupcakes. Caramelise the macadamia nuts, raw sugar and remaining 1 teaspoon maple syrup in a frying pan. Sprinkle over the cupcakes for garnish. Drizzle with more maple syrup to serve.

CAPPUCCINO SEMOLINA CAKE

MAKES ONE 25 CM (10 INCH) LOAF

1½ tsp instant espresso powder
1½ tsp cocoa powder
2½ tbsp hot water
¼ tsp ground cinnamon
80 g (2¼ oz) butter, softened
½ cup (110 g) sugar
¼ cup (55 g) vanilla sugar
1 pinch salt
3 eggs
¼ cup (50 g) semolina
400 g (14 oz) low-fat quark or Greek-style yogurt
200 g (7 oz) cream cheese
¼ cup (60 g) crème fraîche
2 tbsp milk
1 tsp maple syrup

Also:
Butter, for greasing
Fine breadcrumbs, for dusting
150 ml (5 fl oz) single (pure) cream
1–2 tsp icing (confectioners') sugar
Cocoa powder, for dusting

1 Preheat the oven to 160°C (320°F). Butter a 25 cm (10 inch) loaf tin and dust with fine breadcrumbs. Invert the tin and tap lightly to get rid of excess crumbs.

2 Dissolve the instant espresso powder and cocoa powder in the hot water. Mix in the cinnamon. Whisk the butter, sugar, vanilla sugar and salt until creamy, then add the eggs one by one. Stir in the semolina, quark, cream cheese and crème fraîche. Remove about 320 g (11¼ oz) of the batter and combine with the milk. Transfer the batter to the tin, level the surface and freeze for about 15 minutes. Combine the remaining batter with the espresso and cocoa mixture and maple syrup. Carefully pour the batter on top of the semi-frozen batter.

3 Bake for about 65–70 minutes. Switch the oven off and leave the oven door closed. Allow the cake to rest in the hot oven for about 15 minutes. Remove the cake from the oven and set aside to cool completely (this will take at least 2½ hours) before inverting it onto a serving plate.

4 Whip the cream and icing sugar until stiff. Spread all over the cake. Serve dusted with cocoa powder.

LEMON MUFFINS WITH CREAM CHEESE FILLING

MAKES 12

4 small lemons
150 g (5½ oz) cream cheese
100 g (3½ oz) sugar
¼ cup (55 g) vanilla sugar
2 eggs
¾ cup (200 g) plain yogurt (3.5% fat)
⅓ cup (75 ml) canola oil
1½ cups (220 g) plain flour
⅓ cup (30 g) blanched, ground almonds
2 tsp baking powder
1 pinch salt

Also:
Butter, for greasing
Flour, for dusting
1 small lemon
¼ cup (60 g) sugar
Icing (confectioners') sugar, for dusting

1 Preheat the oven to 180°C (350°F). Butter a 12-hole muffin tin and dust with flour. Wash 2 lemons under hot water, pat dry and finely grate the zest. Juice 4 lemons. You'll need about ½ cup (120 ml) juice.

2 Whisk the cream cheese with 2 tablespoons of the lemon juice, 1 tablespoon of the sugar and 1½ tablespoons of the vanilla sugar until creamy. Combine the eggs, yogurt, oil, remaining sugar and vanilla sugar with 90 ml (3 fl oz) of the lemon juice and the lemon zest. Combine the flour, ground almonds, baking powder and salt in a separate bowl and add to the egg mixture.

3 Measure 1 tablespoon of the batter into each muffin hole. Top with each with 1 heaped teaspoon of the cream cheese mixture, then divide the remaining batter on top. Bake the muffins until golden brown, about 22 minutes.

4 Meanwhile, wash the lemon under hot water and pat dry. Use a vegetable peeler or lemon zester to remove fine strips of lemon zest. Bring the sugar to the boil with the remaining lemon juice and simmer for about 10 minutes to thicken to a syrup. Add a little water if necessary.

5 Remove the muffins from the oven, drizzle immediately with the syrup and garnish with the lemon zest. Set aside to cool briefly and then remove from the tin. Dust with icing sugar to serve.

RASPBERRY SOUR CREAM CAKE

MAKES ONE 24 CM (9½ INCH) CAKE

85 g (3 oz) plain flour
1½ tbsp sugar
1½ tbsp vanilla sugar
1 pinch salt
¼ cup (60 g) cold butter, diced
1 egg yolk

For the sponge:
4 eggs, separated
1 pinch salt
100 g (3½ oz) sugar
60 g (2¼ oz) plain flour
50 g (1¾ oz) cornflour
½ tsp baking powder

For the filling:
400 g (14 oz) raspberries
6 gelatine sheets
500 g (1 lb 2 oz) thick sour cream
250 g (9 oz) low-fat quark or Greek-style yogurt
100 g (3½ oz) crème fraîche
2 tbsp orange juice
100 g (3½ oz) sugar
1½ tbsp vanilla sugar
400 ml (14 fl oz) single (pure) cream
2 tbsp icing (confectioners') sugar

Also:
Sugar, for sprinkling
⅓ cup (115 g) strained raspberry jam
250 g (9 oz) white chocolate

1 Combine the flour, sugar, vanilla sugar and salt in a mixing bowl. Rub in the butter until the mixture resembles coarse breadcrumbs. Add the egg yolk and knead everything to combine well. Wrap in plastic wrap and refrigerate for 30 minutes. Preheat the oven to 200°C (400°F) and line a 24 cm (9½ inch) springform tin with baking paper. Roll the dough out into a circle on the plastic wrap. Transfer to the tin and bake for 8 minutes. Leave the oven on.

2 For the sponge, beat the egg whites with the salt and half of the sugar until stiff. Whisk the egg yolks and remaining sugar until light and creamy, about 5 minutes. Carefully fold the egg yolk mixture into the beaten egg whites. Sift the combined flour, cornflour and baking powder over the egg mixture. Fold in gently. Spread the sponge mixture on a baking tray lined with baking paper, about 1.5 cm (⅝ inch) high. Bake for 10–12 minutes. Invert the sponge onto a tea towel sprinkled with sugar. Remove the baking paper, cover the sponge with a damp tea towel and set aside to cool. Slice into strips 6 cm (2½ inches) wide.

3 For the filling, mash the berries with a fork and pass them through a sieve. Soak the gelatine in cold water. Whisk the sour cream, quark, crème fraîche and orange juice with the sugar and vanilla sugar. Transfer the soaked, wet gelatine to a small saucepan. Dissolve over low heat, stirring continuously, then combine with the mashed berries. Stir the berry mixture into the sour cream mixture and refrigerate for 20 minutes. Whip the cream with the icing sugar until stiff.

4 Transfer the pastry base to a serving plate. Spread with 1½ tablespoons of the jam. Place a cake ring around the base. Join two sponge strips to form a circle and line the cake ring. Join more sponge strips to make a larger and a smaller circle so there is 2.5 cm (1 inch) between each circle. Place the sponge circles on the base. Fold half of the whipped cream into the berry mixture. Transfer to a piping bag and carefully pipe it between the sponge circles. Refrigerate the cake and remaining whipped cream for at least 6 hours.

5 Spread the remaining whipped cream on top of the cake so that the sponge circles are covered. Remove the cake ring. Warm the remaining jam and spread it over the top of the cake. Melt the white chocolate and use it to glaze the side. Set aside to dry and refrigerate until serving.

BLACKBERRY GANACHE TARTLETS

MAKES 12

1¾ cups (250 g) plain flour
⅓ cup (80 g) sugar
¼ cup (55 g) vanilla sugar
1 pinch ground cinnamon
1 pinch salt
½ cup (125 g) cold butter
1 egg yolk

For the filling:
200 g (7 oz) dark chocolate
50 g (1¾ oz) milk chocolate
½ cup (125 ml) single (pure) cream
1½ tbsp sugar

Also:
Butter, for greasing
Flour, for dusting
2 cups (250 g) blackberries
Icing (confectioners') sugar, for dusting

1 Combine the flour, sugar, vanilla sugar, cinnamon and salt in a mixing bowl. Dice the butter and rub into the flour until the mixture resembles coarse breadcrumbs. Add the egg yolk and knead everything quickly until well combined. Cover with plastic wrap and refrigerate for 1 hour.

2 Preheat the oven to 180°C (350°F). Butter a 12-hole muffin tin and dust with flour. Invert the tin and tap lightly to get rid of excess flour. Roll out the dough on a lightly floured work surface until 3 mm (⅛ inch) thick. Use a cookie cutter to cut out twelve 10 cm (4 inch) discs. (You can use a tartlet tin to cut the discs and create fluted edges.) Carefully line the muffin holes with the dough and gently press in the edges. Bake for about 15 minutes. Leave to cool completely before carefully removing the tartlet shells from the tins.

3 For the filling, coarsely chop both types of chocolate. Combine the cream and sugar in a saucepan. Bring to the boil, then simmer briefly until the sugar has dissolved. Remove from the heat. Gradually add the chocolate and stir into the hot cream to melt. Set the ganache aside to cool and thicken. Once cooled, spread 3 teaspoons in each tartlet shell.

4 Gently pick through and wash the blackberries and pat dry. Top each tartlet with three blackberries. Serve dusted with icing sugar.

FRUITY NUT BARS

MAKES ABOUT 16

2 tbsp hazelnuts
¼ cup (30 g) walnuts
1½ tbsp almonds
40 g (1½ oz) milk chocolate
25 g (1 oz) marzipan paste
1 tbsp dried cranberries
1 tbsp dried apricots
1 tbsp pistachios, chopped
100 g (3½ oz) butter, softened
¼ cup (55 g) sugar
1½ tbsp vanilla sugar
1 egg
⅔ cup (100 g) plain flour
½ cup (50 g) ground almonds
½ cup (50 g) ground hazelnuts
½ tsp grated orange zest

Also:
⅔ cup (80 g) icing (confectioners') sugar
About ¼ cup (60 ml) Amaretto or orange juice

1 Finely chop the hazelnuts, walnuts and almonds. Grate the milk chocolate and marzipan. Finely chop the cranberries and apricots. Combine everything with the pistachios and set aside.

2 Whisk the butter, sugar and vanilla sugar until light and creamy, then add the egg. Combine the flour, ground almonds, hazelnuts and grated orange zest and quickly stir into the butter mixture. Add the fruit and nut mixture and fold in quickly. Shape the dough into a ball, cover with plastic wrap and refrigerate for at least 45 minutes.

3 Preheat the oven to 170°C (340°F). Roll the dough into a 22 cm (8½ inch) square, about 1.5 cm (⅝ inch) thick, on a sheet of baking paper. Carefully lift the paper and dough onto a baking tray. Bake for about 22 minutes. Set aside to cool briefly.

4 Whisk the icing sugar into the Amaretto and spread the mixture on top of the warm dough. Leave to cool, then cut into bars.

APPLE AND CASHEW PIE

MAKES ONE 24 CM (9½ INCH) PIE

⅓ cup (50 g) cashews or ground hazelnuts
1½ cups (220 g) plain flour
1 pinch salt
⅓ cup (40 g) icing (confectioners') sugar
150 g (5½ oz) cold butter
1 egg yolk

For the filling:
100 g (3½ oz) marzipan paste
3 eggs
150 g (5½ oz) low-fat quark or Greek-style yogurt
100 g (3½ oz) crème fraîche
¼ cup (60 g) sugar
1½ tbsp vanilla sugar
Grated zest of ½ lemon

For the topping:
3 red apples
½ tsp sugar
2 tbsp lemon juice
2½ tbsp cashews
1 tsp raw sugar

Also:
Butter, for greasing
Flour, for dusting
Ground cinnamon, for dusting

1 Finely grind the cashews in a blender. Combine the flour, ground cashews, salt and icing sugar. Dice the butter and rub into the flour mixture until the mixture resembles coarse breadcrumbs. Add the egg yolk and knead everything quickly to make a smooth dough. Shape the dough into a ball, cover with plastic wrap and chill for at least 30 minutes.

2 Meanwhile, finely grate the marzipan and combine with all of the other ingredients for the filling.

3 Core the apples for the topping and cut into 2 mm (1/16 inch) slices. Bring some water to the boil in a wide saucepan. Add the sugar, lemon juice and sliced apples and simmer the apples for a few minutes until soft. Remove and set aside to cool. Layer the sliced apples, overlapping slightly, and roll up to make rose shapes. Chop the cashews.

4 Preheat the oven to 180°C (350°F). Butter a 24 cm (9½ inch) loose-based pie tin and dust with flour. Invert the tin and tap lightly to get rid of excess flour. Roll out the dough on a lightly floured surface into a circle about 5 mm (¼ inch) thick. Transfer the dough to the pie tin. Pour the filling mixture into the pie shell, leaving a little gap on top. (You may have a little filling left over, depending on how deep your tin is.) Arrange the apple roses on top, starting from the outside and working into the centre. Sprinkle the cashews and raw sugar over the top of the pie.

5 Bake the pie until golden brown, about 35–40 minutes. Set aside to cool, then remove from the tin and serve dusted with cinnamon.

COCONUT CAKE

MAKES ONE 18 CM (7 INCH) CAKE

6 eggs, separated
1 pinch salt
150 g (5½ oz) sugar
1½ tbsp vanilla sugar
125 g (4½ oz) plain flour
⅓ cup (40 g) cornflour

For the cream:
280 ml (9½ fl oz) coconut milk
¾ cup (70 g) desiccated coconut
200 g (7 oz) white chocolate
2 tbsp orange juice
1 tsp grated orange zest
1 cup (250 g) mascarpone
300 g (10½ oz) low-fat quark or Greek-style yogurt
75 g (2½ oz) icing (confectioners') sugar

Also:
Butter, for greasing
About ½ cup (165 g) strained raspberry jam
About 1¾ cups (100 g) flaked coconut
Fresh raspberries, for garnish

1 Preheat the oven to 180°C (350°F) and butter two 18 cm (7 inch) springform tins. Line the bases with baking paper. Beat the egg whites and salt until stiff. Whisk the egg yolks, sugar and vanilla sugar until thick and creamy. Combine the flour and cornflour. Quickly stir into the egg yolk mixture in three batches, alternating with half of the beaten egg whites. Gently fold in the remaining egg whites. Divide the batter between the tins and smooth the tops. Bake for about 25 minutes. Remove from the oven and set aside to cool before removing the cakes from the tins. Leave to cool completely.

2 For the cream filling, heat the coconut milk and desiccated coconut over low heat. Simmer to reduce for about 30 minutes, stirring occasionally, until the mixture takes on a thick porridge consistency. Meanwhile, chop the white chocolate. Remove the saucepan from the heat and gradually add the chocolate, orange juice and orange zest. Stir to melt the chocolate. Refrigerate the mixture for 20 minutes.

3 Whisk the mascarpone and quark until creamy. Mix in the icing sugar. Stir in the coconut mixture and refrigerate for at least 1 hour until the cream has firmed up.

4 Halve the sponge cakes horizontally Place one sponge base onto a serving plate, cut side up. Spread with raspberry jam. Follow with just under a quarter of the coconut cream mixture. Spread the cut side of the second sponge base with jam and gently place on top of the cream, jam side down. Spread the top with raspberry jam and just under another quarter of the coconut cream mixture. Repeat with the remaining two sponge bases. Spread the remaining coconut cream on top of the cake and around the sides. Decorate with flaked coconut and garnish with fresh raspberries.

CRÈME BRÛLÉE TARTLETS WITH MULLED WINE PEARS

MAKES ABOUT 8

For the pastry:
1⅓ cups (200 g) plain flour
½ cup (50 g) ground almonds
¼ cup (50 g) sugar
1½ tbsp vanilla sugar
½ tsp ground cinnamon
1 pinch salt
½ cup (125 g) cold butter
1 egg yolk

For the filling:
1 vanilla bean
4 egg yolks
¼ cup (50 g) sugar
300 ml (10½ fl oz) single (pure) cream
100 ml (3½ fl oz) milk

For the mulled wine pears:
3 pears
200 ml (7 fl oz) red wine
¼ cup (50 g) sugar
1 cinnamon stick
2 cloves
¼ tsp ground cardamom
1 pinch ground ginger
1 orange

Also:
Butter, for greasing
Flour, for dusting
¼ cup (45 g) brown sugar

1 Start preparing the mulled wine pears the day before. Peel and halve the fruit and remove the cores. Place the red wine, sugar and spices into a wide saucepan. Peel and juice the orange. Add the peel and juice to the pan. Bring to the boil, then simmer over low heat for 8 minutes. Strain the mixture through a sieve. Discard the spices and orange peel and return the wine to the saucepan. Bring to the boil and add the pears. Simmer until soft, about 10 minutes. Remove from the heat and leave to cool. Leave the pears to marinate in the refrigerator overnight.

2 For the pastry, combine the flour, ground almonds, sugar, vanilla sugar, cinnamon and salt in a mixing bowl. Dice the butter and rub into the flour until the mixture resembles coarse breadcrumbs. Add the egg yolk and knead everything until well combined. Shape the dough into a ball, cover with plastic wrap and chill for at least 30 minutes.

3 For the filling, split the vanilla bean lengthwise and scrape out the seeds. Whisk the egg yolks and sugar until thick and creamy, about 5 minutes. Combine the cream, milk, vanilla seeds and empty pod in a saucepan and bring to the boil. Take off the heat, remove the vanilla pod and whisk the cream and milk mixture into the egg yolks, stirring continuously. Leave to cool.

4 Preheat the oven to 190°C (375°F). Butter eight 10 cm (4 inch) tarlet tins and dust with flour. Roll out the pastry dough about 3 mm (⅛ inch) thick on a lightly floured surface. Line the tins with the pastry. Prick the bases all over with a fork and bake for about 10 minutes. Remove from the oven and divide the cooled filling among the bases (you may have some filling left over, depending on the depth of the tins). Reduce the oven to 140°C (275°F). Bake the tartlets for another 35–40 minutes.

5 Remove the tartlets from the oven and set aside to cool. Carefully unmould, then refrigerate for at least 1 hour. Sprinkle the tops evenly with brown sugar. Use a kitchen torch to caramelise the sugar and create a golden crust. Remove the pears from the liquid and drain well. Thinly slice into fans and arrange on top of the tartlets.

PLUM AND POPPYSEED CRUMBLE

MAKES ONE 26 CM (10½ INCH) PIE

1⅓ cups (200 g) plain flour
¾ cup (80 g) ground almonds
⅓ cup (70 g) sugar
½ tsp ground cinnamon
1 pinch salt
100 g (3½ oz) cold butter
1 egg yolk

For the filling:
600 ml (21 fl oz) milk
150 ml (5 fl oz) single (pure) cream
200 g (7 oz) ground poppyseeds
½ cup (70 g) custard powder
125 g (4½ oz) sugar
2 tsp grated lemon zest
500 g (1 lb 2 oz) plums

For the crumble:
⅔ cup (100 g) plain flour
80 g (2¾ oz) butter, softened
80 g (2¾ oz) brown sugar
2 tsp ground poppyseeds
¼ tsp ground cinnamon

Also:
Butter, for greasing
Flour, for dusting
Dried beans, for blind baking

1 Combine the flour, ground almonds, sugar, cinnamon and salt in a mixing bowl. Dice the butter. Add to the dry ingredients along with the egg yolk and 2–3 tablespoons cold water. Knead to make a smooth dough. Shape the dough into a ball, cover with plastic wrap and chill for 30 minutes.

2 Preheat the oven to 180°C (350°F). Butter a 26 cm (10½ inch) springform tin and dust with flour. Invert the tin and tap lightly to get rid of excess flour.

3 Roll out the dough on a lightly floured surface into a circle large enough to line the base and side of the tin. Carefully transfer the dough to the tin. Line the base with baking paper and top with dry beans. Blind bake for about 15 minutes. Remove the paper and beans and set aside to cool. Leave the oven on.

4 For the filling, whisk all the ingredients except the plums together in a saucepan until the custard powder has dissolved. Bring to the boil, then simmer, stirring continuously, until thick. Remove from the heat and set aside to swell for a few minutes. Leave to cool. Meanwhile, wash the plums and pat dry. Remove the stones and quarter the fruit.

5 For the crumble, rub the flour together with the butter, sugar, poppyseeds and cinnamon in a mixing bowl.

6 Spread the filling over the base and level the top. Spread the plums evenly on top and sprinkle with the crumble mixture. Bake until golden brown, about 45 minutes. (If you like a crunchier crumble, switch the oven to the grill function for the last few minutes of cooking.) Remove the pie from the oven and leave it to cool in the tin before carefully transferring it to a serving plate to cool completely. Refrigerate for at least 3 hours, preferably overnight, before slicing.

The Princess and the Pea

AIRY DELIGHTS

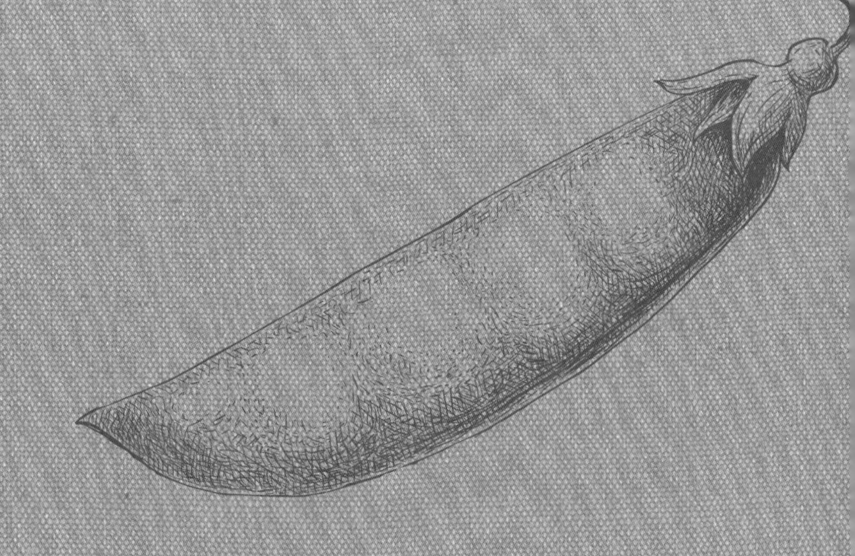

Once there was a Prince...

...who wanted to marry a Princess. Only a real one would do. So he travelled through all the world to find her, and everywhere things went wrong. There were Princesses aplenty, but how was he to know whether they were real Princesses? There was something not quite right about them all. So he came home again and was unhappy, because he did so want to marry a real Princess.

One evening a terrible storm blew up. It lightened and thundered and rained. It was really frightful! In the midst of it all came a knocking at the town gate. The old King went to open it.

Who should be standing outside but a Princess, and what a sight she was in all that rain and wind. Water streamed from her hair down her clothes into her shoes, and ran out at the heels. Yet she claimed to be a real Princess.

'We'll soon find that out,' the old Queen thought to herself. Without saying a word, she went to the bedchamber, stripped back the bedclothes, and put just one pea in the bottom of the bed. Then she took twenty mattresses and piled them on the pea. Then she took twenty eiderdown feather beds and piled them on the mattresses. Up on top of all these the Princess was to spend the night.

In the morning they asked her, 'Did you sleep well?'

'Oh!' said the Princess. 'No. I scarcely slept at all. Heaven knows what's in that bed. I lay on something so hard that I'm black and blue all over. It was simply terrible.'

They could see she was a real Princess and no question about it, now that she had felt one pea all the way through twenty mattresses and twenty more feather beds. Nobody but a Princess could be so delicate. So the Prince made haste to marry her, because he knew he had found a real Princess.

As for the pea, they put it in the museum. There it's still to be seen, unless somebody has taken it.

There, that's a true story.

CREAM PUFFS WITH BERRY COMPOTE

MAKES ABOUT 22

For the choux pastry:
½ cup (125 ml) milk
½ cup (125 g) butter
1 pinch salt
1¼ cups (180 g) plain flour
1½ tbsp sugar
5 eggs
1 tsp baking powder

For the Chantilly cream:
1 vanilla bean
400 ml (14 fl oz) cream
50 g (1¾ oz) icing (confectioners') sugar

For the compote:
500 g (1 lb 2 oz) mixed berries
⅓ cup (75 g) sugar
1 cup (250 ml) blackcurrant juice
2 tbsp cornflour
Zest of ½ lemon

Also:
Icing (confectioners') sugar, for dusting

1 For the pastry, add the milk, butter and salt to a shallow saucepan together with ½ cup (125 ml) water. Bring to the boil. Combine the flour and sugar and add to the boiling milk mixture at once, stirring continuously with a wooden spoon. Continue to stir until the mixture forms a ball and starts to come away from the side of the pan. A white layer will form on the bottom of the saucepan.

2 Preheat the oven to 200°C (400°F) and line two baking trays with baking paper. Transfer the hot dough ball to a mixing bowl and combine with 1 egg. Set aside to rest briefly, then gradually add the remaining eggs, one by one, until you have a smooth, thick mixture. Stir the baking powder in last. Transfer the pastry to a piping bag with a star nozzle and pipe 4 cm (1¼ inch) rounds onto the baking paper, spacing them a little apart. Bake for about 22–24 minutes until golden brown, one tray at a time. (Do not open the oven before the pastry is cooked, and do not underbake the pastry, or it will collapse after baking.) Remove from the oven and leave to cool completely on a wire rack. Once cool, use kitchen scissors or a sharp serrated knife to slice off the top third.

3 For the Chantilly cream, split the vanilla bean lengthwise. Scrape out the seeds and set the empty pod aside. Whip the cream until stiff, gradually adding the icing sugar. Stir in the vanilla seeds. Refrigerate the cream mixture.

4 For the compote, wash and pick over the berries, halving any larger ones. Place in a bowl. Caramelise the sugar in a small saucepan until light brown, stirring continuously. Deglaze with the blackcurrant juice. Add the vanilla pod and simmer over low heat for about 5 minutes to dissolve the caramel and reduce the mixture. Whisk the cornflour into a little water. Stir into the simmering mixture to thicken. Remove the vanilla pod, add the lemon zest and pour the mixture over the berries. Stir carefully to combine, cover and leave to cool.

5 Fill the cream puffs with the cream and the berry compote. Top with the lids and dust with icing sugar. Serve immediately.

MINI CINNAMON ROLLS

MAKES 8

1⅔ cups (250 g) plain flour
1½ tbsp sugar
1½ tbsp vanilla sugar
¼ tsp salt
10 g (¼ oz) fresh yeast
100 ml (3½ fl oz) lukewarm milk
100 g (3½ oz) cold butter
1½ tbsp plain yogurt (3.5% fat)

For the filling:
70 g (2½ oz) brown sugar
1½ tbsp vanilla sugar
1½ tsp ground cinnamon
1 pinch ground cardamom

Also:
Flour, for dusting

1 Combine the flour, sugar, vanilla sugar and salt in a mixing bowl. Make a well in the centre. Crumble the yeast into the well and add half of the lukewarm milk. Stir the milk and yeast together with a little flour from around the edge. Cover the bowl with plastic wrap and leave until the yeast mixture develops bubbles, about 30 minutes.

2 Meanwhile, melt a quarter of the butter and leave to cool a little. Thinly slice the remaining butter and return to the refrigerator. Whisk the remaining milk into the yogurt and add to the yeast mixture, along with the melted butter. Knead everything together until well combined, about 5 minutes. Cover the dough again and leave to rise for 1 hour.

3 Roll out the dough on a lightly floured surface to a 25 cm (10 inch) square, about 8 mm (⅜ inch) thick. Cover half of the dough entirely with the sliced butter, leaving a 1.5 cm (⅝ inch) edge. Fold the other half of the dough over and press the edges together to seal. Gently roll the dough out again to a larger rectangle, being careful not to squeeze out any of the butter. Fold first one, then the other short side in towards the middle. You'll end up with a piece of dough with three layers. Refrigerate the folded dough for about 45 minutes. Roll out again to a rectangle about 25 x 35 cm (10 x 14 inches) in size and 5 mm (¼ inch) thick.

4 Preheat the oven to 190°C (375°F) and line a baking tray with baking paper. For the filling, combine the brown sugar with the vanilla sugar, cinnamon and cardamom. Sprinkle the mixture evenly over the dough, leaving a narrow edge all around. Roll the dough up tightly from the long side closest to you. Cut the roll into eight even pieces. Transfer to the baking tray, spacing them a little apart. Use the handle of a wooden spoon to push down firmly along the centre of the dough pieces so that the rolls fan up on the sides.

5 Bake the rolls for about 15–20 minutes until golden brown. Remove from the oven and leave to cool on a wire rack.

TIRAMISU CAKE

MAKES ONE 20 CM (8 INCH) CAKE

2 eggs, separated
85 g (3 oz) sugar
1½ tbsp warm water
3 tsp butter
½ cup (70 g) plain flour
2 tsp cocoa powder
¼ tsp baking powder
1 pinch salt

For the espresso ganache:
2½ tbsp single (pure) cream
1 tbsp Amaretto
1 tsp instant espresso powder
80 g (2¾ oz) dark chocolate, coarsely chopped
50 g (1¾ oz) milk chocolate, coarsely chopped

For the cream:
1 cup (250 g) mascarpone
1 large egg
¼ cup (60 g) sugar
3 gelatine sheets
1½ tbsp Amaretto
150 ml (5½ fl oz) single (pure) cream
1½ tbsp vanilla sugar
1 tsp grated orange zest

Also:
Butter, for greasing
Flour, for dusting
220 g (7¾ oz) savoiardi biscuits
50 g (1¾ oz) dark chocolate
Cocoa powder, for dusting

1 Preheat the oven to 180°C (350°F). Butter a 20 cm (8 inch) springform tin and dust with flour. Additionally, line the base of the tin with baking paper. Whisk the egg yolks, sugar and water until thick and foamy, about 5 minutes. Melt the butter and leave to cool a little before stirring into the batter. Combine the flour, cocoa powder, baking powder and salt. Sift the mixture over the wet ingredients and stir in. Beat the egg whites until stiff and fold into the batter. Transfer the batter to the tin and bake for about 20 minutes. Set aside to cool, remove the base from the tin and leave to cool completely on a wire rack. Transfer the base onto a serving plate. Place a cake ring around the base.

2 For the ganache, bring the cream, Amaretto and instant espresso powder to the boil. Remove from the heat and stir in the chocolate to melt. Spread half the ganache across the base, being careful not to spread it to the edge, as this will cause the cake ring to stick. Refrigerate the base for about 20 minutes.

3 Meanwhile, whisk the mascarpone for the cream until smooth. Place the egg and sugar into a bowl over a saucepan of simmering water and whisk until thick and creamy, about 5 minutes. Remove from the heat. Soak the gelatine in cold water. Gently warm the Amaretto in a small saucepan. Squeeze excess water lightly from the gelatine and stir the gelatine into the Amaretto to dissolve. Whisk the gelatine mixture into the warm egg mixture. Fold in the mascarpone. Whip the cream and vanilla sugar until stiff and gently fold into the mascarpone mixture with the orange zest. Refrigerate for 20 minutes until the cream is lightly set. Spread half the cream over the sponge base. Refrigerate for 15 minutes.

4 Top the cream filling with a layer of tightly packed savoiardi biscuits. Spread with the remaining ganache and refrigerate for 15 minutes. Top with the remaining cream filling. Refrigerate for 2 hours.

5 Melt the dark chocolate. Spread thinly on a sheet of baking paper and refrigerate to set. Break into small flakes. Remove the cake ring by carefully sliding a sharp knife dipped in hot water around the edge. Dust the cake with cocoa powder and garnish with the chocolate flakes. Trim the remaining savoiardi biscuits to the height of the cake and line the outside of the cake with biscuits.

CINNAMON COOKIES

MAKES ABOUT 20

2 egg whites
1 pinch salt
140 g (5 oz) icing (confectioners') sugar
120 g (4¼ oz) plain flour
½ cup (50 g) blanched, ground almonds
1 tsp ground cinnamon
¼ tsp ground cardamom
1 tsp cocoa powder
1 tsp grated lemon zest

Also:
Flour, for dusting
Hundreds and thousands, for sprinkling

1 Beat the egg whites and salt until semi-stiff. Gradually whisk in the icing sugar and continue to whisk until you have a firm mixture with glossy peaks. Transfer about 4 tbsp of the beaten egg whites to a small bowl and set aside.

2 Combine the flour, ground almonds, cinnamon, cardamom, cocoa powder and lemon zest and fold into the egg whites. Wrap the dough with plastic wrap and refrigerate for 30 minutes.

3 Preheat the oven to 160°C (320°F) and line a baking tray with baking paper. Roll out the dough about 3 mm (⅛ inch) thick on a lightly floured surface and use a cookie cutter to cut out 5 cm (2 inch) circles. Knead the leftover dough together and repeat. Transfer the cookies onto the baking tray. Use a teaspoon to spread thinly with the reserved egg whites and sprinkle with hundreds and thousands.

4 Bake the cookies for about 15 minutes. Remove from the oven and leave to cool a little on the tray, then transfer to a wire rack and leave to cool completely.

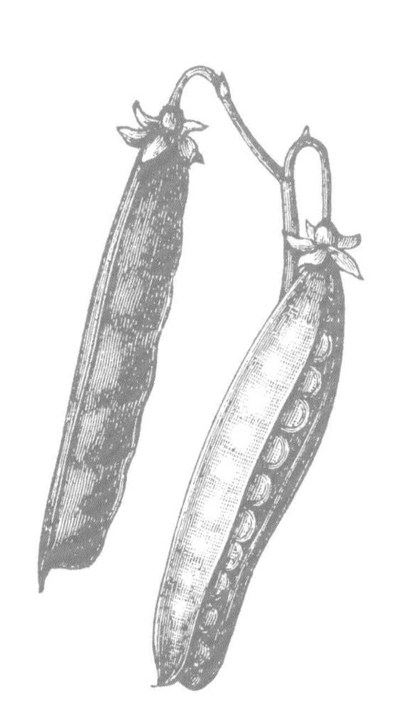

MANGO AND CHOCOLATE SQUARES

MAKES ABOUT 25

For the sponge:
3 eggs, separated
1 pinch salt
⅓ cup (75 g) sugar
60 g (2¼ oz) plain flour
¼ cup (25 g) cornflour
¼ cup (25 g) cocoa powder
1½ tsp baking powder

For the filling:
1 large ripe mango or 300 g (10½ oz) frozen diced mango
5 gelatine sheets
⅓ cup (80 ml) pineapple juice
250 g (9 oz) low-fat quark or Greek-style yogurt
100 g (3½ oz) cream cheese
100 g (3½ oz) crème fraîche
⅓ cup (70 g) sugar
150 ml (5 fl oz) single (pure) cream
1½ tbsp vanilla sugar

Also:
Butter, for greasing
Flour, for dusting
100 g (3½ oz) dark chocolate
1 tsp coconut oil

1 Preheat the oven to 200°C (400°F). Butter a 24 cm (9½ inch) square cake tin and dust with flour. Invert the tin and tap lightly to get rid of excess flour.

2 For the sponge, beat the egg whites until stiff, gradually adding the salt and sugar. Stir in the egg yolks and 2 tablespoons cold water. Combine the flour, cornflour, cocoa powder and baking powder. Gently fold into the egg mixture in three batches. Divide the batter in half, transfer one half to the tin and level the top. Bake the sponge for about 10 minutes, leave to cool briefly, then gently invert to remove from the tin. Repeat with the second half. Trim the edges straight, if necessary.

3 For the filling, peel and dice the mango. Soak 2 of the gelatine sheets in cold water. Simmer the diced mango and pineapple juice in a small saucepan for about 10 minutes to reduce. Remove from the heat and blend. Squeeze out excess water from the gelatine and stir into the slightly cooled mango purée to dissolve. Refrigerate for 15 minutes.

4 Soak the remaining gelatine in cold water. Place a cake ring around the sponge base. Spread with the puréed mango, level the top and refrigerate for about 30 minutes. Meanwhile, whisk the quark, cream cheese, crème fraîche and sugar to combine. Lightly squeeze out the gelatine and dissolve in a saucepan over low heat. Stir ¼ cup (60 ml) of the quark mixture into the gelatine, then add the gelatine mixture to the remaining quark and mix to combine. Refrigerate for about 20 minutes.

5 Meanwhile, whip the cream and vanilla sugar until stiff and fold into the cream mixture as it sets. Spread the quark mixture on top of the mango layer and top with the second sponge cake. Refrigerate for at least 4 hours, preferably overnight.

6 Cut the cake into 4 cm (1½ inch) squares. Chop the chocolate and melt it over a saucepan of simmering water together with the coconut oil. Leave to cool a little, then spread or drizzle it over the mango and chocolate squares. Secure the squares with toothpicks if needed.

MOCHA CUPCAKES

MAKES 12

3 eggs, separated
⅔ cup (140 g) sugar
150 g (5½ oz) butter, softened
1½ tbsp vanilla sugar
2 tbsp freshly brewed espresso, cooled
125 g (4½ oz) ground hazelnuts
⅔ cup (100 g) plain flour
2 tsp cocoa powder
¼ tsp baking powder
1 pinch ground cinnamon
12 chocolate coffee beans

For the topping:
1 tbsp cream cheese
1 tbsp instant espresso powder
1 cup (250 g) mascarpone
½ cup (60 g) icing (confectioners') sugar
Chocolate coffee beans, for garnish

1 Preheat the oven to 180°C (350°F). Line a 12-hole muffin tin with paper cases.

2 Beat the egg whites until semi-stiff. Gradually add 100 g (3½ oz) of the sugar and continue to beat until stiff. Whisk the butter, remaining sugar and vanilla sugar in a separate mixing bowl until foamy. Add the egg yolks one at a time, then stir in the espresso.

3 Combine the nuts, flour, cocoa powder, baking powder and cinnamon. Add to the beaten egg whites, along with the egg yolk mixture. Gently fold with a spatula until well combined.

4 Divide the batter evenly among the muffin holes. Push a chocolate coffee bean inside each cupcake. Bake for 20–23 minutes. Use a toothpick to test for doneness (see page 10). Set the cupcakes aside to cool completely before removing them from the tin.

5 For the topping, warm the cream cheese in a small saucepan and stir in the espresso powder to dissolve. Leave to cool. Whisk the mascarpone and icing sugar until creamy. Stir in the espresso cream cheese. Transfer to a piping bag with a large round nozzle and pipe on top of the cooled cupcakes. Garnish with chocolate coffee beans.

FOREST BERRY ICE CREAM CAKE

MAKES ONE 24 CM (9½ INCH) CAKE

For the base:
180 g (6 oz) wholemeal digestive biscuits
½ cup (120 g) butter
⅓ cup (40 g) ground hazelnuts
1 tbsp caster sugar

For the filling:
3 large eggs, separated
1 cup (125 g) icing (confectioners') sugar
1 vanilla bean
400 g (14 oz) quark (20% fat) or Greek-style yogurt
Grated zest and juice of 1 lemon
1 cup (250 ml) single (pure) cream

For the topping:
2 cups (250 g) mixed frozen berries, thawed
⅓ cup (75 ml) blackcurrant juice
1½ tbsp sugar
1–2 tsp cornflour
Honey, to taste

Also:
Fresh berries, to serve

1 For the base, transfer the digestive biscuits to a resealable plastic bag and finely crush with a rolling pin. Melt the butter and combine with the biscuit crumbs, ground hazelnuts and sugar. Line the base of a 24 cm (9½ inch) springform tin with baking paper. Spread the biscuit mixture evenly over the base and press down with the back of a spoon. Freeze for about 30 minutes.

2 For the filling, whisk the egg yolks and icing sugar in a bowl set over a saucepan of simmering water and whisk until thick and creamy, about 5 minutes. Leave to cool. Split the vanilla bean lengthwise and scrape out the seeds. Combine the quark with the vanilla seeds, lemon zest and juice. Beat the egg whites until stiff. Whip the cream until stiff. Gently fold first the quark mixture, then the beaten egg whites and finally the whipped cream into the cooled egg yolk mixture. Transfer to the tin, cover and freeze for 3 hours.

3 For the topping, purée the berries using a stick blender. Strain into a small saucepan through a fine sieve. Add the blackcurrant juice and sugar and bring to the boil, stirring. Simmer to reduce for about 5 minutes. Whisk the cornflour into a little cold water. Stir into the berry mixture and simmer to reduce for 1–2 minutes, stirring continuously. Sweeten with honey, to taste. Leave the berry mixture to cool completely before spreading on top of the filling. Return the cake to the freezer for at least another 2 hours.

4 Transfer the cake to the refrigerator for about 30 minutes before serving. To serve, dip a sharp knife into hot water and slide it around the inside of the tin. Transfer the cake to a serving plate and slice, repeatedly dipping the knife into hot water. Serve with fresh berries.

CHOCOLATE AMARANTH THINS

MAKES 20–24

¼ cup (55 g) butter
½ cup (80 g) plain flour
¼ cup (20 g) blanched, ground almonds
⅔ cup (80 g) icing (confectioners') sugar
1½ tbsp vanilla sugar
2 tbsp cocoa powder
½ tsp ground cinnamon
2 large egg whites

Also:
About 5 tbsp popped amaranth

1 Preheat the oven to 180°C (350°F) and line two baking trays with baking paper.

2 Melt the butter and leave to cool a little. Combine the flour, ground almonds, icing sugar, vanilla sugar, cocoa powder and cinnamon. Add the egg whites and butter and stir to make a thick batter.

3 Use a 6 cm (2½ inch) cookie cutter or portioning ring to spread very thin, even circles of batter (about 1 tsp batter per circle) onto the trays. (Alternatively, the batter can also be spread quite easily without a ring with moistened hands. This is easiest if you draw the circles onto the baking paper beforehand.) Sprinkle each thin with popped amaranth.

4 Bake the thins for about 8 minutes. Leave on the trays to cool completely, then carefully separate them from the baking paper.

MINI LIME PIE WITH RASPBERRY MERINGUE

MAKES ONE 20 CM (8 INCH) PIE

1¼ cups (185 g) plain flour
1 pinch salt
2 tbsp sugar
100 g (3½ oz) cold butter
1 egg yolk, whisked with 3 tsp cold water

For the lime filling:
⅔ cup (140 g) sugar
⅓ cup (40 g) cornflour
⅓ cup (75 ml) lime juice
2 egg yolks
25 g (1 oz) butter
Grated zest of 2 small limes

For the raspberry meringue:
1 cup (125 g) fresh raspberries
1 cup (125 g) icing sugar
2 egg whites

Also:
Butter, for greasing
Flour, for dusting
Dried beans, for blind baking

1 Combine the flour, salt and sugar. Dice the butter and rub into the flour until the mixture resembles coarse breadcrumbs. Add the whisked egg yolk and knead everything quickly to combine well. Grease a 20 cm (8 inch) loose-based pie tin. Roll out the dough about 4 mm (3/16 inch) thick on a lightly floured surface. Line the pie tin with the dough. Prick the dough all over with a fork and chill for about 20 minutes.

2 For the lime filling, combine the sugar and cornflour with 225 ml (7½ fl oz) water in a small saucepan and whisk until smooth. Whisk in the lime juice and egg yolks and bring the mixture to the boil, stirring continuously. Be careful not to burn it. Simmer the lime mixture over low heat for about 5 minutes until thick. Stir in the butter and lime zest and take the saucepan off the heat.

3 Preheat the oven to 200°C (400°F). Line the pie base with baking paper and top with dry beans. Blind bake the base for about 15 minutes, then remove the paper and beans. Bake the base for another 3 minutes until the edges start to brown. Reduce the oven to 170°C (340°F).

4 Pick over the raspberries. Rinse gently and pat dry. Mash 1 heaped cup of the berries finely with a fork, pass through a sieve and remove the seeds. Set aside the remaining berries. Stir ¼ cup (30 g) of the icing sugar into the raspberry purée. Whisk the egg whites until semi-stiff, then gradually add the remaining icing sugar. Continue to beat for about 8 minutes until glossy peaks start to form and the mixture is quite firm. Mix in the raspberry purée in several batches.

5 Spread the filling in the pastry case to come just under the edge. Top with the reserved raspberries. Spread the raspberry meringue on top of the pie using a palette knife and shape into a flat dome. Transfer to the oven and bake for about 20 minutes.

SPICED MACARONS

MAKES ABOUT 25

¾ cup (85 g) blanched, ground almonds
140 g (5 oz) icing (confectioners') sugar
1 pinch ground cinnamon
2 egg whites
1 tbsp caster sugar
Powdered food coloring

For the white chocolate filling:
60 g (2¼ oz) white chocolate
25 ml (¾ fl oz) single (pure) cream
1 pinch ground cardamom
1 tsp very finely chopped pistachios

For the milk chocolate filling:
60 g (2¼ oz) milk chocolate
25 ml (¾ fl oz) single (pure) cream
½ tsp ground cinnamon
1 tsp very finely chopped hazelnuts

For the dark chocolate filling:
60 g (2¼ oz) dark chocolate
25 ml (¾ fl oz) single (pure) cream
1 pinch ground allspice
1 pinch chilli powder

1 Preheat the oven to 150°C (300°F) and line a baking tray with baking paper. Grind the almonds very finely in a blender, along with the icing sugar and cinnamon. (The finer the mixture, the smoother the macaron surfaces will be.) Pass the almond mixture through a fine sieve.

2 Whisk the egg whites until stiff, gradually adding the sugar. Add enough food coloring, if using, to color the batter as desired. Next, very gently fold the almond mixture into the whisked egg whites in five batches to make a smooth, viscous batter. Do not stir and be careful not to overmix so that the macarons will turn out beautifully light. Transfer the batter to a piping bag with a small, round nozzle and pipe 2.5 cm (1 inch) circles onto the baking paper, spacing them a little apart.

3 Leave the piped batter to rest and dry for about 30 minutes, then carefully transfer the tray to the bottom rack in the oven. Use a wooden spoon to keep the oven door ajar during baking to allow moisture to escape. Bake the macarons for about 15 minutes. Remove from the oven and leave to cool completely on the tray.

4 For the first filling, coarsely chop the white chocolate and slowly melt in a bowl set over a saucepan of simmering water together with the cream, stirring frequently. Do not let the water get too hot. Stir in the cardamom and pistachios. For the second filling, melt the milk chocolate with the cream. Stir in the cinnamon and chopped hazelnuts. For the third filling, melt the dark chocolate with the cream and combine with the allspice and chilli. Leave the fillings to cool and refrigerate for at least 30 minutes.

5 Next, spread the fillings on half of the baked circles. Carefully top each circle with another half and press gently together. Set the macarons aside to dry. Serve on a platter or tiered cake stand.

MINI GINGERBREAD KUGELHOPFS

MAKES 12

125 g (4½ oz) honey
1½ tbsp sugar
1½ tbsp vanilla sugar
115 g (4 oz) butter
2 eggs
1½ cups (225 g) plain flour
1 tbsp cocoa powder
1 tsp ground ginger
1½ tsp baking powder
1 pinch salt
¼ cup (60 g) candied ginger
2 tsp grated lemon zest
¼ cup (40 g) chopped almonds
125 g (4½ oz) apricot jam

Also:
Butter, for greasing
Flour, for dusting
About 100 g (3½ oz) marzipan paste, for garnish (optional)
Icing (confectioners') sugar, for dusting

1 Add the honey, sugar, vanilla sugar and butter to a small saucepan. Heat until the sugar and butter have melted, stirring continuously. Transfer the mixture to a bowl and set aside to cool.

2 Preheat the oven to 180°C (350°F). Butter a 12-hole mini kugelhopf tin and dust with flour. Invert the tin and tap lightly to get rid of excess flour.

3 Stir the eggs into the honey mixture one by one. Combine the flour, cocoa powder, ginger, baking powder and salt and quickly stir into the honey mixture. Finely dice the candied ginger and fold into the batter, along with the lemon zest and chopped almonds.

4 Transfer the batter to the tin, filling each hole about three-quarters full. (This is best done using a piping bag.) Bake for 17–20 minutes. Use a toothpick to test for doneness (see page 10).

5 Meanwhile, warm the jam. Set the mini kugelhopfs aside to cool briefly, then remove from the tin and brush with the jam while still warm. Roll out the marzipan, if using, and cut out tiny stars using a very small cookie cutter or star-shaped piping nozzle. Garnish the cakes with the marzipan and dust with icing sugar.

BLUEBERRY CLAFOUTIS

1 Preheat the oven to 180°C (350°F). Grease a 24 cm (9½ inch) pie tin and dust with flour. Invert the tin and tap lightly to get rid of excess flour. Gently pick through and wash the blueberries and pat dry.

2 Beat the egg whites until stiff, gradually adding half of the sugar. Whisk the egg yolks, vanilla seeds, cinnamon, lemon zest, remaining sugar and salt until creamy. Combine the flour and ground almonds. Whisk together the cream and milk. Stir the flour and cream mixtures into the egg yolk mixture in batches, alternating between the two. Gently fold in the beaten egg whites in three batches. Finally, fold the blueberries into the batter.

3 Transfer the batter to the pie tin and bake for about 30 minutes. If the top browns too quickly, cover the clafoutis with foil for the last 10 minutes of baking. Remove the clafoutis from the oven and leave to cool a little, then generously dust with icing sugar. Combine the crème fraîche with the honey and lemon zest. Serve with the warm clafoutis.

MAKES ONE 24 CM (9½ INCH) PIE

1 cup (150 g) fresh blueberries
3 eggs, separated
85 g (3 oz) sugar
Seeds of 1 vanilla bean
1 pinch ground cinnamon
½ tsp grated lemon zest
1 pinch salt
½ cup (75 g) plain flour
¼ cup (25 g) ground almonds
⅓ cup (75 ml) single (pure) cream
⅓ cup (75 ml) full-cream milk

Also:
Butter, for greasing
Flour, for dusting
Icing (confectioners') sugar, for dusting
150 g (5½ oz) crème fraîche
1–2 tbsp honey
½ tsp grated lemon zest

INDEX

A

B

C

N

O

P

Q

R

THANKS

My thanks go to everybody who has supported, advised, encouraged and critiqued me as this cookbook evolved – above all Sophie, whose limitless enthusiasm never failed to inspire me. Without you, this book would not exist. A big thank you also to Dagmar and Angela for your confidence in me, and to Kathrin for your sharp eyes.

Thank you also to Yelda for your fabulous photography. Your photographic sensitivity and perfection are beyond words!

A huge thank you to my parents, Lars, Tim, Stefan, Susan, Lauritz, Emil and Ida for their honest critique, and to our neighbours in Eicklingen, who tirelessly nibbled their way through the entire book. More thanks to Sigrid and Jochen, who patiently taste-tested my recipes every time they passed through on their way from Heidelberg to Silesia or back.

Thank you to my dear Janna. It might only have taken me half the time to bake some of the cakes without you, but you are still my favorite baking buddy. Your childlike delight in weighing ingredients, rolling out doughs and cutting out cookies is a marvel in itself. I bet that you will be a master baker in only a few years' time.

Thank you to Gunnar for simply everything. I know that you generally prefer a good steak to a piece of cake. Yet you graciously and patiently suffered the chaos that I created in our kitchen on an almost daily basis for weeks and months. I promise there won't be any more sweets for a while. At least a little while. You are the best.

And finally, thanks to my little Enno. I'm grateful simply for your existence – what an incredible delight! This book is for you.

CHRISTIN GEWEKE is a freelance cookbook editor and has previously worked as an editor with various publishers. She is not only a dedicated writer, but also a passionate baker who is quite happy to spend any free minute in the kitchen trying out new cake recipes. She lives in the German countryside near Celle together with her husband, daughter, son and cat.

YELDA YIMAZ started out with analogue photography and studied photography and visual communications/media at Hamburg University of Fine Arts. She loves cooking and baking, meeting new people and exploring new places – and filling books with her experiences. In 2014, she created the Hamburg Food Swap, where people from all walks of life come together over a shared dinner to taste and exchange recipes and home-made delicacies.

© 2018 Hölker Verlag, in Coppenrath Verlag GmbH & Co. KG

First Skyhorse Publishing edition 2019.

Originally published in German in 2018 by Hölker Verlag, and in English in 2019 as *Fairytale Baking* by Murdoch Books.

All Rights Reserved. No part of this book may be reproduced in any manner without the express written consent of the publisher, except in the case of brief excerpts in critical reviews or articles. All inquiries should be addressed to Skyhorse Publishing, 307 West 36th Street, 11th Floor, New York, NY 10018.

Skyhorse Publishing books may be purchased in bulk at special discounts for sales promotion, corporate gifts, fund-raising, or educational purposes. Special editions can also be created to specifications. For details, contact the Special Sales Department, Skyhorse Publishing, 307 West 36th Street, 11th Floor, New York, NY 10018 or info@skyhorsepublishing.com.

Skyhorse® and Skyhorse Publishing® are registered trademarks of Skyhorse Publishing, Inc.®, a Delaware corporation.
Visit our website at www.skyhorsepublishing.com.

10 9 8 7 6 5 4

Library of Congress Cataloging-in-Publication Data is available on file.

Recipe development: Christin Geweke
Photography: Yelda Yilmaz
Cover illustration: Heidrun Schröder
Layout and typesetting: Stefanie Wawer
Editor: Sophie Schwaiger
Pre-press: FSM Premedia, Munster

Publisher: Corinne Roberts
Translator: Claudia McQuillan-Koch (excepting stories, translated by Edgar Taylor and Marian Edwardes)
English-language editor: Justine Harding
Production director: Lou Playfair

Cover design by Daniel Brount
Cover artwork: Getty Images

Hardcover ISBN: 978-1-5107-5181-1
Ebook ISBN: 978-1-5107-5554-3

Printed in China